Revolution

Key Concepts in Political Science

GENERAL EDITOR: Leonard B. Schapiro

EXECUTIVE EDITOR: Peter Calvert

Other titles in the same series include:

ALREADY PUBLISHED

IN PREPARATION

Revolution

Peter Calvert
University of Southampton

Praeger Publishers
New York · Washington · London

Praeger Publishers, Inc.
111 Fourth Avenue, New York, N.Y. 10003, U.S.A.
5 Cromwell Place, London s.w.7, England
Published in the United States of America in 1970
by Praeger Publishers, Inc.

Library of Congress Catalog Card Number: 77–95664

Printed in Great Britain

Contents

'Key Concepts'
an Introductory Note

Political concepts are part of our daily speech—we abuse 'bureaucracy' and praise 'democracy', welcome or recoil from 'revolution'. Emotive words such as 'equality', 'dictatorship', 'élite' or even 'power' can often, by the very passions which they raise, obscure a proper understanding of the sense in which they are, or should be, or should not be, or have been used. Confucius regarded the 'rectification of names' as the first task of government. 'If names are not correct, language will not be in accordance with the truth of things', and this in time would lead to the end of justice, to anarchy and to war. One could with some truth point out that the attempts hitherto by governments to enforce their own quaint meanings on words have not been conspicuous for their success in the advancement of justice. 'Rectification of names' there must certainly be: but most of us would prefer such rectification to take place in the free debate of the university, in the competitive arena of the pages of the book or journal.

Analysis of commonly used political terms, their reassessment or their 'rectification', is, of course, normal activity in the political science departments of our universities. The idea of this series was indeed born in the course of discussion between a few university teachers of political science, of whom Professor S. E. Finer of Manchester University was one. It occurred to us that a series of short books, discussing the 'Key Concepts' in political science would serve two purposes. In universities these books could provide the kind of brief political texts which might be of assistance to students in gaining a fuller understanding of the terms which they were constantly using. But we also hoped that outside the universities there exists a reading public which has the time, the curiosity and the inclination to pause to reflect on some of those words and ideas which are so often taken for granted. Perhaps even 'that insidious and crafty animal', as Adam Smith described

7

the politician and statesman, will occasionally derive some pleasure or even profit from that more leisurely analysis which academic study can afford, and which a busy life in the practice of politics often denies.

It has been very far from the minds of those who have been concerned in planning and bringing into being the 'Key Concepts' series to try and impose (as if that were possible!) any uniform pattern on the authors who have contributed, or will contribute, to it. I, for one, hope that each author will, in his own individual manner, seek and find the best way of helping us to a fuller understanding of the concept which he has chosen to analyse. But whatever form the individual exposition may take, there are, I believe, three aspects of illumination which we can confidently expect from each volume in this series. First, we can look for some examination of the history of the concept, and of its evolution against a changing social and political background. I believe, as many do who are concerned with the study of political science, that it is primarily in history that the explanation must be sought for many of the perplexing problems of political analysis and judgement which beset us today. Second, there is the semantic aspect. To look in depth at a 'key concept' necessarily entails a study of the name which attached itself to it; of the different ways in which, and the different purposes for which, the name was used; of the way in which in the course of history the same name was applied to several concepts, or several names were applied to one and the same concept; and, indeed, of the changes which the same concept, or what appears to be the same concept, has undergone in the course of time. This analysis will usually require a searching examination of the relevant literature in order to assess the present stage of scholarship in each particular field. And thirdly, I hope that the reader of each volume in this series will be able to decide for himself what the proper and valid use should be of a familiar term in politics, and will gain, as it were, from each volume a sharper and better-tempered tool of political analysis.

There are many today who would disagree with Bismarck's view that politics can never be an exact science. I express no opinion on this much debated question. But all of us who are students of politics—and our numbers both inside and outside the universities continue to grow—will be the better for knowing what precisely we mean when we use a common political term.

London School of Economics
and Political Science

Leonard B. Schapiro
General Editor

for my mother

Acknowledgements

It is a great pleasure here to have the opportunity to thank Derick Mirfin for the idea which led to the writing of this book and for his invitation to help launch the series. I should also like to express my thanks to Liam O'Sullivan for his understanding criticism and to my students at the University of Southampton for their questions and comments. I am most grateful to Diana Marshallsay, for providing the index, to Michael ffolliott-Foster for editorial encouragement and assistance, and to Miss Pat Cox and Miss Harriet Tatman for typing and photocopying. All errors of fact, or idiosyncrasies of interpretation, are my responsibility alone.

1/Revolution in the Ancient World

Modern anthropologists recognize political organization as being 'concerned with the control and regulation of the use of physical force'.[1] The state is defined by the presence of regulations governing the use of physical force. These regulations may be of various kinds; physical force may be employed to redress wrongs, but only under rules laid down by custom. At the boundary of the state the government of custom ceases. Beyond that boundary the unrestricted use of force is permissible in the settlement of disputes.

There is, however, one use of force which is explicitly excluded from this definition, but which is of the highest importance in the understanding of political organization. This is what may broadly be termed 'revolution'. In popular usage today revolution is a blanket term covering a number of possible uses of physical force, which are not regarded as being legal in the strict sense, but which may nevertheless be customary within the area of the state, for the purpose of promoting political change.[2]

Here 'revolution' may be understood throughout as referring to events in which physical force (or the convincing threat of it) has actually been used successfully to overthrow a government or regime. Where such movements have not been successful, they are referred to, according to context, as 'rebellions', 'revolts', 'insurrections' or 'uprisings'. Though there are semantic variations between these terms, the usage of each follows custom, and does not imply a value judgement.

In examining the evolution of the concept of revolution one must go back a very long way. Revolution is one of the few political concepts of which we can speak before the era of the ancient Greeks. In fact, it may even be said that it was the first of all political concepts to be recognized as such. The reason for this lies in the limitations imposed by oral tradition in primitive societies. A primitive society living in a state of social order becomes conscious of that social order only when it is interrupted for some reason. To that extent, therefore, the concept of the state cannot be made fully real until the concept of social dissolution or revolution has first been encountered.

The problem in isolating such a concept, however, is the relationship of secular concepts of political power to religious authority. To primitive man the secular world was but part of an overarching cosmic order. The deeds of the gods in the other world, which affected the secular world, were in effect part of that world and could not be differentiated from it. The use of divine sanctions, therefore, to uphold government, could be countered only by the use of the sanctions of an alternative deity or an alternative view of the cosmic order. In the city states of ancient Mesopotamia rivalry between the states was regarded as being the earthly expression of rivalry between city gods in the Assembly of the Gods.[3] We cannot therefore speak of a concept of revolution in these struggles, for the Assembly of the Gods was seen as being an open forum, and the rivalry of states as being one between different entities. Only when violence can be seen as occurring within one entity can we speak of it as revolution.

The origin of the concept

For this reason, the concept of revolution must be seen as originating, not in ancient Mesopotamia, but in ancient Egypt. The invention of writing was practically contemporary with the unification of the North and the South, in approximately 3200 BC. It is a sad commentary on human nature that one of writing's first, and as far as we are concerned still one of its principal uses, was to record the number of human beings slain in the succession of internal wars that followed.[4] Pre-dynastic Egypt had consisted of two states, each consisting of people who regarded themselves as 'the followers of Horus'. Whether or not these people were a new race that had recently moved into the Nile valley is still disputed by archaeologists. The wars of unification began with the ascendancy of the North, the area of the delta, but unification was in fact achieved by a Southern king, known to future generations as Menes. The regime which Menes and his successors established was dual in character, with separate establishments for North and South Egypt, and it is clear that during the reigns of weak kings rival rulers tended to appear, for some considerable time, in the delta region. These revolts, though undoubtedly considered by the rulers of united Egypt to be rebellious in character, cannot be regarded as being truly revolutionary in view of the dual nature of the state.

Some two hundred years after the unification there occurred a change of dynasty, the first of many such changes, the precise nature of which is not known today. Under the kings of the Second Dynasty it seems clear that the indigenous people of Egypt, whose god, Set, had been vanquished by the followers of Horus, had increased in strength and numbers. In consequence, King Sekhemib abandoned the worship of Horus for the worship of the enemy god. This significant change obviously accompanied a period of religious and political upheaval which may have included the burning of the tombs of his predecessors to destroy their chances of an after life. At the end of the dynasty order was restored by the strong king Khasekhem. Stone vessels from his reign are inscribed 'the year of fighting the northern enemy within the City of Nekheb'. On these vessels the city is represented by its goddess holding a circle inscribed with the word 'rebels' (*Besh*).[5] If these rebels are identical with the 'northern enemies' referred to on a statue of the same ruler, the slaughter amounted to the astonishing total of 47,209. The worship of Horus was re-established, together with the united monarchy, and both, in principle at least, were to endure down to the days of the Roman Empire.

Clearly the identification of the concept of rebellion is an important stage on the way to an identification of revolution. But monuments of this period, and almost all writings that have survived from ancient Egypt, were of a more or less official character. Revolutionary manifestos, if they existed, were probably in the temporary form of graffiti written with paint or chalk. Nor do we know precisely of what the worship of Set consisted, or whether it was in any way inferior or superior to that of Horus. What we do know is that before Egyptian history had really started, the structure of the new state had already had to cope with three phenomena all of which at separate times have been subsumed under the general heading of revolution. These were the palace revolt, or change of ruler; insurrection, or rebellion; and social, i.e. religious reform accompanied by violence.

At the end of the Sixth Dynasty power in Egypt collapsed almost completely, the chief cause being the weakening of central power under an aged ruler, and the rise of the power of the hereditary rulers of the forty-two provinces or *Nomes*. These hereditary rulers, or *Nomarchs*, struggled among themselves for ascendancy and the re-establishment of strong centralized authority in Egypt was eventually achieved by the Nomarch of Thebes, in about 2100 BC. The period of stable rule that followed is known as the Middle Kingdom, and the Middle Kingdom is the period of highest literary value in Egyptian history. It would be strange indeed if this period had not taken account of the political significance of some at least of the events which had shaped its past.

The earliest recorded description of political change occurring through violence appears to be the account of the assassination of King Amenemhat I, approximately 1962 BC. The description of this incident, representing a dream in which the dead king was supposed to have given advice to his son and successor, became a favourite theme for literary composition in Egyptian schools.

It was after supper when night was come, I took an hour of repose, lying upon my bed. I was tired and my heart began to follow sleep. Of a sudden weapons were brandished and there was talk concerning me, whilst I remained like a snake of the desert. I awoke to find, being by myself. I found it was an attack by the guard. Had I hastened with weapons in my hand, I could have driven back the caitiffs. But there is none strong at night. None can fight alone. There is no successful issue without a protector.[6]

In this particular instance, the normal rules of succession to the throne were in fact followed. The king's son, absent from the capital on a campaign in Syria, received news upon the road. He left the camp immediately and in secret for the capital, where he succeeded in asserting his control within a brief period. A member of his entourage, who happened to be present when he received the news, was so frightened by it that he fled to the desert. The story of his adventures, like the text of the king's advice itself, became a popular subject for literary repetition for future generations.[7]

The message of these compositions was twofold. Those about the dead king, suggested that rebellion was motivated by ingratitude and a desire for personal aggrandizement. The theme of the second genre was that the king's kindliness and justness to those who followed him loyally was such, that they could count upon the very highest reward. In secular terms, this meant that the traditions of society placed a strong emphasis on stability and authority, powerfully reinforced by the theocratic nature of the absolute monarchy and the role of the gods in human affairs. Rebellion was not only politically unjustifiable, it was also sacrilege. Under the later period of Egyptian history, known as the New Empire, this meant that the collapse of the weak Nineteenth Dynasty was long delayed, and eventually achieved only at the hands of the high priest.

Significantly, Amenemhat, as the founder of a new powerful dynasty endowed it with an institution not previously known in Egyptian history. This was the standing army, organized under leaders in companies of a hundred. We do not know what the total strength of this army was, but it is clear that the rebellion in which he perished occurred among members of his own bodyguard. Under the New Empire, the army functioned for the first time as an arbiter of political affairs at the close of the Eighteenth Dynasty, when it took the leading role in putting an end to the religious authority of the reign of Akhnaten (*c.* 1379–62 BC) and subsequently installed its commander, Haremhab, on the throne as the first king of the Nineteenth Dynasty.

Between the Middle Kingdom and the New Empire there lay a second period of social dissolution known to modern historians as the Second Intermediate Period. Once more, government failed, and the country relapsed into a state of division and anarchy. Like the First, the Second Intermediate Period is so imperfectly documented that in its assessment successive generations have shown a strong tendency to impose upon it their own interpretation and their own essentially modern ideas of revolution. This is misleading, for although their judgement may well be right, it cannot be said to be so with any degree of confidence. Modern Egypt does bear very striking resemblances to all that is known of the Egypt of the Pharaohs, and yet the political ideas by which it is governed are Muslim in origin. Deductions from them as to a specifically 'oriental' quality in ancient Egyptian life are to be distrusted. So, though there are periods in the history of Islamic Egypt in which monarchs followed each other with extreme rapidity, leaving very little impact on the political order, we cannot be certain that this is in fact what happened in these earlier times.

The impact of social upheaval

What we can be certain of, is that the degree of social upheaval experienced in these years was so great that it left a permanent impact on the thought of later ages. In consequence, the concept of social dissolution must be seen as material to the high degree of centralization that occurred in later ages of Egyptian history, and the increasing emphasis on the unreasoning acceptance of the authority of the state. The description of what Gardiner termed a 'real revolution', to be found in Leiden Papyrus 344, is familiar in its variety of horrors. The papyrus has not been ascribed with certainty to the First Intermediate Period rather than to the Second, and the mention of foreign invaders which it includes is more typical of the later rather than the earlier. The general state of social upheaval, however, which it pictures is undeniably drawn with graphic skill.

> Forsooth, [men's] hearts are violent. Plague is throughout the land. Blood is everywhere. Death is not lacking [?]. The mummycloth [?] speaks, before ever one comes near it [?]. Forsooth, many dead men are buried in the river. The stream is a sepulchre and the place of embalment has become a stream. Forsooth the wealthy are in mourning. The poor man is full of joy. Every town says: let us suppress the powerful among us.

Examples are given of the plight of the former aristocracy.

> Forsooth, gold and lapis lazuli, silver and malachite, carmelian and bronze, . . . are fastened on the necks of female slaves. Good things are in the land. [Yet] the mistresses of houses say: would that we had something to eat. Forsooth, . . . noble ladies. Their limbs are in sad plight by reason of [their] rags.

Gardiner, in selecting some of these quotations, comments that they might 'reflect the distorted vision of a die-hard aristocrat', but he goes on to say that 'there are others describing the political confusion of the times, the dissolution of the laws, and the destruction of public offices and records which cannot well be so construed. Even the person of the king seems to have been subjected to violence, though the sentence where this appears to be stated is of not quite certain interpretation'.[8]

It seems reasonable to accept that the Intermediate Periods were times of social revolution, in that violence was used in the displacement of individuals and groups within the state by others formerly deprived of political advantage. The precise assessment of the extent to which this took place is distorted by the element of foreign invasion alluded to in the Leiden Papyrus. The importance of this element would have been the greater in that the Egyptians had not previously been accustomed, owing to their geographical position, to such incursions.

In any case, the over-all effect was to cut short the development of Egyptian civilization, and to impose upon it the formalization of the traditional pattern of resistance to further change. So great did this resistance become that in the late period of the New Empire the rituals of three thousand years remained sufficiently strong and established to be applicable in turn to dynasties of Libyans, Ethiopians, Persians, and, at length, Greeks. With the respect accorded to antiquity in the ancient world, as in the modern, the concept of rigid stability passed into the political consciousness of Greece. And the role of the divine monarchy of Egypt was accepted directly by Cambyses of Persia and later by Alexander the Great.

Undoubtedly political considerations played an important role in the so-called 'religious revolution' of Akhnaten. The god Amon had become so powerful that his priests held the tenure of the land of the greater part of the country. His word was law and his approval was necessary even for acts of the divine monarch. The bold introduction of a new state religion, the worship of Aton, a universal, non-anthropomorphic god, however much motivated by purely ethical and metaphysical considerations, was bound to have a disruptive effect on the structure of society. The reign of Akhnaten dissolved in chaos, and ended with the dissolution of the greater part of the empire. Order was restored by the former general Haremhab, of whom mention has already been made. His methods combined firmness with justice, and rigid control of the restored aristocracy. 'His Majesty took council with his heart how he might expel evil and suppress lying. The plans of His Majesty were an excellent refuge, repelling violence and delivering the Egyptians from the oppressions which were around them. Behold, His Majesty spent the whole time seeking the welfare of Egypt, and searching out instances of oppression in the land.'

Tax collectors were singled out for special care.

> If the poor man has made for himself a boat with its sail, and, in order to serve the state, has loaded it with the government dues, and has been robbed of the boat, the poor man stands bereft of his property and stripped of his many labours. This is wrong, and the Pharaoh will suppress it with his excellent measures. If there be a poor man who pays the taxes to the two deputies and he be robbed of his property and his boat, my majesty commands that every officer who collects the taxes and takes the boat of any citizen, this law should be executed against him, and his nose should be cut off, and he should be sent in exile to Tharu.[9]

It was, as one might have expected entirely in accordance with Egyptian tradition to see unbending justice as a cure for social discontent. Authority lay in righteousness, and righteousness in the absence of wrong-doing. The sacred book of the Ancient Egyptians, the so-called *Book of the Dead*, had as its key passage the 'Negative Confession,' 'in which the dead man secured his passage to the other world by the correct recitation of a series of denials of specific wrongful acts. So important was the exact observance of the law, that it was held that a mistake by the scribe in the sacred scroll might condemn the dead man to an eternity of wandering or destruction at the hands of monsters of the other world'.[10]

For the commoner, the religion of the other world was of the most profound significance. Only the educated classes might have read the treatise of Amenemhat or the admonitions of Ipuwer, the observer of social chaos. But all knew that the other world was presided over by the god Osiris. Osiris was the divine founder of Egypt, who was treacherously put to death by Set, and it was by avenging his death that the god Horus acquired his particular role as the originator and protector of the Egyptian monarchy. Plutarch, who recorded the story of Osiris for the Greeks of his time, said in the course of his commentary:

> This much may be depended upon: the religious rites and ceremonies of the Egyptians were never instituted upon irrational grounds, never built upon mere fable and superstition, but founded with a view to promote the morality and happiness of those who were to observe them, or at least to preserve the memory of some valuable piece of history or to represent to us some of the phenomena of nature.

The story of Osiris inculcated both abhorrence of rebellion against the monarch, and the disturbance of the divine order which accompanied it. Each of these acts endangered the whole future of the country.[11]

The importance of Egyptian experience

As the Egyptians were distinctively and uniquely nationalistic, it is appropriate that among them should have originated the first of the 'wars of national liberation'. This was the war against the foreign invaders of Egypt during the Second Intermediate Period. These invaders, known to us as the Hyksos ('Shepherd Kings') supplied a line of rulers who assumed the titles and dignities of the former kings. Very little is known about them beyond the fact that they ruled with great cruelty, and made use of calculated terror as a means of instilling obedience in the rebellious populace. Tradition says that they ruled for more than four hundred years. In Breasted's words 'the influence upon Egypt of such a foreign dominion, including both Syria–Palestine and the Lower Nile Valley, was epoch making, and had much to do with the fundamental transformation which began with the expulsion of these aliens. It brought the horse into the Nile Valley and taught the Egyptians warfare on a large scale. Whatever they may have suffered, the Egyptian owed an incalculable debt to their conquerors'.[12]

The war of national liberation appears to have been touched off by the attempt of the Hyksos ruler, Apophis, to suppress one of the leading Egyptian nobles, Sekenenre. He sent a message to Thebes, several hundred miles away, which said: 'One has come to thee concerning the Pool of the Hippotami which is in the City. For they permit me no sleep, day and night the noise of them is in my ear.'[13] It soon became apparent that this was a pretext for getting Sekenenre to come to the Hyksos capital. Sekenenre appears to have decided on revolt; at least, it is clear that he received the support of others in the war which lasted for many years and ended in the expulsion of the foreigners, perhaps some twenty years later.

As with other people in modern times, the Egyptians did not regard this type of war as being a revolution. They regarded it as a war against a foreigner and therefore a foreign war, although it was fought on the soil of Egypt. All references to it, therefore, treated it as such and describe it in the terms normally reserved for warfare of this kind. We are therefore left with the conclusion that revolution to the ancient Egyptians was regarded officially and generally as being rebellion, and therefore wrong. It was, however, sufficiently commonplace to be frequently referred to in inscriptions, and to be made the subject of documents which sought to instil respect for the monarchy, and for the state and the religion which was part of it.

It has already been mentioned that the concept of the divine kingship, and the view of rebellion and revolt that accompanied it, passed to both the Persian and the Macedonian empire. Recently some anthropologists have suggested that this influence upon ancient empires may not have been its most enduring contribution. They point to the widespread prevalence of divine kingship in African societies, along an arc stretching from the Sudan to modern Nigeria. They observe that these kingdoms have a cultural tradition which includes the working of metals and the maintenance of a type of religion very similar to that of the ancient Egyptians. It is, however, argued by others that there is no clear evidence that this similarity is due to a spread from Egypt southwards; rather, that Egypt may have been influenced by the hinterland.[14] At least we know that a similar form of state organization existed in the Nubian kingdoms of Meroe and Napata, and may therefore have been influential in North Africa as late as the third century of our own era. Shinnie points to an inscription describing the revolt of the Noba against the Nubian King Aezanes (c. AD 325–75), as proof that the kingdom of Meroe had already collapsed. It is for us a reminder that the nature of revolt and the attitude of authority towards it tends to remain constant over time.

The Egyptian experience, as far as the West is concerned, was less important for the impact it had on Aristotle's thinking than in the important role that Egypt played as the scene of power politics in the East during the last few centuries before Christ. As recorded in the histories of Herodotus, the fall of an Egyptian ruler was an historical event much like any other. He spoke of it in value-free terms and hence his comments were capable of being received in a very matter-of-fact way. Two examples are particularly relevant here. The first is the case of the overthrow of Apries, the Pharaoh Hophra of the Bible. Apries was overthrown by his leading general Amasis after a military conspiracy in which Amasis had gained considerable support. The king, hearing that the revolt was in progress, hastily and summarily ordered the general's ear and nose to be cut off. 'The rest of the Egyptians, who still adhered to him', writes Herodotus, 'seeing one of the most distinguished among them treated in so unworthy a manner, did not delay a moment, but went immediately over to the others and gave themselves to Amasis'. Apries was thereupon summarily strangled.[15]

Herodotus also describes the cause of the successful revolt against Smerdis of Persia, which put Darius on the throne. Smerdis himself was said to be a usurper, having seized the throne secretly on the death of Cambyses. The conspirators prepared their plot without Darius, and subsequently invited him to join them. Darius rejected their plan for a public revolt in favour of a quick *coup d'état*. He did so on the grounds that the government's intelligence system was too good for any open conspiracy to survive for long. On the other hand, the rank of the conspirators was sufficiently high to enable them to gain access to the palace and therefore for their plot to have a very fair chance of success. As Darius had predicted, they were able to pass the doorkeeper successfully and, once inside, to strike down all who opposed them.[16]

Darius was thereupon proclaimed king on the strength of an omen.

Those lessons of revolution which made particular impact on the ancient world were quite straightforward. Revolution represented a reversion to the primitive practice of sacrificing a weak ruler when he had outlived his usefulness. The weak ruler was replaced by a strong one, the act of replacement itself serving to confirm that divine disfavour had fallen upon the overthrown ruler, and favour on the ruler who had defeated him. Since strength did not exist in the physical ability of the king alone to defend himself, but in the loyalty of his bodyguard and soldiery, strict controls were imposed by wise rulers on their closest retainers. At Meroe, the bodyguard of the king was sacrificed on his death, whether that death occurred from natural causes or otherwise. Clearly, such a practice ensured a high degree of alertness among the bodyguard in the defence of the monarch on whom their lives depended. Thus, it seems, Meroe avoided the development of a praetorian guard with political power, such as that which later was to arise in Rome.

The concept of legitimation received strength and reinforcement from the existence of revolt and revolution. In Egypt, the title to the throne was conveyed through the female line, and the legitimation of the ruler occurred through marriage to the person carrying the right of sovereignty. This served very effectively on, for example, the fall of the Eighteenth Dynasty when Haremhab married the heiress to the throne. A later, and more celebrated example, was the transfer through marriage to Cleopatra of the claim to the Egyptian throne to the Julio–Claudians. Legitimation could be alternatively, or simultaneously, conferred by divine recognition, a recognition which lay in the hands in the priest of the god to give or to withhold. In general, the existence of a stable priesthood holding political power implied a desire for political stability, and the equation between stability and the giving of justice was reinforced by the fact that justice meant religious observance, and hence donation of worldly goods to the priesthood. It was left to the Greeks, knowing forms of government other than monarchy, to argue that revolutionary activity had other purposes and other consequences.

2/Plato, Aristotle and the Romans

Greek history and revolution

Most of the early Greek states were originally monarchies. It has been suggested that monarchy was not native to the Greeks, but had been acquired, in the course of their wanderings, from their observations of forms of government normal elsewhere. Homer described such a monarchy, where in the absence of a king no executive action could be taken.[1] By the time of written historical evidence, however, these early monarchies were being either limited or terminated by the commercial aristocracy. This limitation or termination gave rise not only to oligarchical and even democratic forms of government, but also to the age of tyranny. The tyrant was a man who ruled on his own authority where the aristocracy had proved too weak to hold the reins of power and his methods of achieving power were often abrupt and informal.

To the world of classical Greece, therefore, revolution was a concept that embodied both the change of rulers implied in the palace revolt, and the social displacement implied by the rise of an aristocracy or the fall of aristocratic exclusiveness. In the mobile Greek society, where forms of government varied considerably over a small area, and consciousness of them was enhanced by the creation of colonies and the establishment of cities modelled on their founders, changes of government were bound to be regarded with an almost personal degree of involvement. But such changes had also a wider implication. They took place in a diplomatic environment dominated by the proximity of the Persian Empire, and so bore a crucial relationship to the degree of independence possible for other states. Thus the displacement of an oligarchy by a democracy meant the acquisition of a possible ally against Persia; the reverse, the possibility of a further extension of Persian power and a threat to other states.

The first contribution of the Greeks to the concept of revolution, therefore, lay in their history. For the first time, revolutionary events were subject to detailed scrutiny. This scrutiny revealed clearly the relationship between political change and the social dissolution that was all too likely to accompany or to follow it. It is often believed, and was indeed stated by Arthur Hatto in his celebrated monograph on the concept of revolution, that the Greeks could not have appreciated the concept of total revolution as exhibited, for example, in the French Revolution of 1789. Yet it would be hard for a reader of Thucydides' *The Peloponnesian War* not to admit that in his account of the revolution in Corcyra he had come very close to it.

The oligarchy of Corcyra was supported by the Corinthians, but was disliked by its own citizens, who inclined towards Athens. When the Corinthians tried to aid the oligarchy to increase its control, the attempt at repression drove a small group to attempt the desperate measure of breaking into the Council and stabbing the leader of the oligarchy and some sixty others. They then called an assembly to justify themselves. The oligarchy counter-attacked with the aid of a Corinthian trireme, but were only able to secure the harbour, while the democratic party held and fortified the Acropolis. Unable to dislodge them, and beaten in the resumed fighting, the oligarchs fired the city, but the timely arrival of an Athenian fleet saved the democrats, and, once free, they fell upon the oligarchs and massacred them.

'So savage was the progress of this revolution, and it seemed all the more so because it was one of the first which had broken out', wrote Thucydides. 'Later, of course, practically the whole of the Hellenic world was convulsed, with rival parties in every state—democratic leaders trying to bring in the Athenians, and oligarchs trying to bring in the Spartans.' In short, 'in time of war, when each party could always count upon an alliance which would do harm to its opponents and at the same time strengthen its own position, it became a natural thing for any-one who wanted a change of government to call in help from outside'.[2]

The importance of such diplomatic involvement in our own time is all too obvious. But for Thucydides the major lesson was what happened to men and ideas in a situation of rapid change accompanied by violence. The dissolution of the state (*stasis*), translated as 'revolution', led to a complete reformulation of the basic social relationships of individuals. In the process, the integrity of Greek society perished, to the ultimate advantage only of the men who sought to control it for their own purposes.

So revolutions broke out in city after city, and in places where the revolutions occurred late the knowledge of what had happened previously in other places caused still new extravagances of revolutionary zeal, expressed by an elaboration in the methods of seizing power and by unheard-of atrocities in revenge. To fit in with the change of events, words, too, had to change their usual meanings. What used to be described as a thoughtless act of aggression was now regarded as the courage one would expect to find in a party member; to think of the future and wait was merely another way of saying one was a coward; any idea of moderation was just an at-tempt to disguise one's unmanly character; ability to understand a question from all sides meant that one was totally unfitted for action. Fanatical enthusiasm was the mark of a real man, and to plot against an enemy behind his back was perfectly legitimate self-defence. Anyone who held violent opinions could always be trusted, and anyone who objected to them became a suspect. . . . As for the citizens who held moderate views, they were destroyed by both the extreme parties, either for not taking part in the struggle or in envy at the possibility that they might survive.[3]

It was indeed fortunate that by the time these events came about, the Greeks had already begun a serious and remarkably successful attempt to understand the workings of the political system.

On the one hand, they developed a clear theory of the state, differentiating its parts by function. In their experimentation with constitutional law they distinguished from the beginning between the magistrates, the council and the assembly, and related the functioning of each to the social classes that achieved fullest expression through them. Furthermore, they studied the interaction between the elements that composed the institutions of government, in terms of the social division between the people on the one hand and the nobles on the other. And they also had to develop a theory of political change, and in this theory violence had an important place.

Plato's organic concept

In likening the changes in political structures to the ebb and flow of nature, Plato laid the foundations for that organic concept of political systems which is found today in the work of Talcott Parsons. In an allegory of growth and decay, he postulated the emergence of a constitution at a stage which he called 'the timocratic'. (To him this meant a state governed by men whose primary motivation was love of honour. In the Aristotelian sense it refers to a polity with property qualifications for the rulers.) The timocratic state represented what in his day was the most primitive surviving form of Greek political system, that of Sparta. It is important to note that he saw the constitution as a defined bargain between rival groups, and that for him the drawing up of a constitution represented the point at which the state emerged from pre-constitutional order.

The timocratic state, Plato believed, would tend, because of its imperfectly defined status, to evolve into oligarchy, thence to democracy and ultimately to tyranny. In broad terms, this was in fact the course of Greek political development down to the time at which Plato wrote. Though the over-all process of evolution might take a very long time, it is clear that he saw individual episodes in the process of change as potentially violent. Groups holding power were not likely to yield it unless challenged by the use of force, and in fact such overt uses had already occurred. Realistically, he saw that a similar cycle could be initiated in his ideal state, the 'Republic', through usurpation by the auxiliaries whose job it was to defend it. Such usurpation could only be avoided by the maintenance of absolute standards of justice and a proper balance between the powers that composed the state.

Plato is, therefore, the true founder of the study of military intervention in politics. But he is better known, by all accounts, by the fact that, in his discussion of tyranny, he gave prominence to the economic role of the 'capitalists' evolved under the form of democratic government. These men he expected to be overthrown by gangs of desperadoes concerned only with their own good, so in turn creating the perfectly unjust society. This perfectly unjust society was the precise opposite of what his ethical values demanded of a state, and it was therefore the state which was most marked by internal violence and the most liable to violent political intervention.[4]

The Aristotelian analysis

Further than this, Plato did not go. It was left to the father of the study of comparative government, Aristotle, to establish the first comprehensive basis for the study of revolution. Revolution forms the subject of the whole of Book v of *The Politics*.[5] Aristotle, of course, accepted the principle of the state; that is to say, he accepted the principle that political order could not exist without it. But he recognized that ordinary states are founded upon erroneous ideas of justice and that these erroneous and incomplete ideas lead directly to discontent and upheaval. Such upheaval, though it may not manifest itself in violent form, may yet alter the form of the state to such an extent that the effects of its government are completely different. For him, therefore, revolution is not an exceptional phenomenon, but a necessary fact of political change. It is a political phenomenon, both violent and non-violent, representing the fundamental process of change which leads to the alteration or displacement of social groupings.

Aristotle approached the problem of revolution from the standpoint of one having a clear idea of what the state was. For him, monarchy was not the only form of government. In fact, to a Greek, it was a form of government which was archaic and in many respects weakened by inherent flaws. The forms of government more common in the Greek world, democracy and oligarchy, however, were no more perfect, though they differed from monarchy in important respects which made the possibilities of political change within them substantially different. In all cases, Aristotle saw the prime cause of revolution as being inequality. Inequality took different forms according to the nature of the government.

> Democracy, for example, arises out of the notion that those who are equal in any respect are equal in all respects; because men are equally free, they claim to be absolutely equal. Oligarchy is based on the notion that those who are unequal in one respect are in all respects unequal; being unequal, that is, in property, they suppose themselves to be unequal absolutely. The democrats think that as they are equal they ought to be equal in all things; while the oligarchs under the idea that they are unequal claim too much, which is one form of inequality. All these forms of government have a kind of justice, but, tried by an absolute standard, they are faulty; and, therefore, both parties, whenever their share in the government does not accord with their preconceived ideas, stir up revolution.[6]

The prime cause of revolution, inequality, therefore, manifests itself in different states in different ways. These immediate causes Aristotle classified in two groups, which one may broadly regard as being psychological and social respectively. In the 'psychological' one can find the desire for gain or honour; insolence; fear; love of superiority; contempt, or, indeed, the jealousy caused by the disproportionate increase in some part of the state. Of a different sort, he rightly perceived, were such immediate 'social' factors as the existence of electoral intrigues; carelessness among the ruling élite; neglect by them of trifling matters giving rise to discontent; and the dissimilarity of the elements within the state, as, for example, when two tribes fell out.

The modernity of Aristotle's ideas is remarkable, though it is sometimes disguised by the instances that he gives.

> In revolutions, the occasions may be trifling, but great interests are at stake. Trifles are most important when they concern the rulers, as was the case of old at Syracuse for the Syracusan constitution was once changed by a love-quarrel of two young men, who were in the government. The story is that while one of them was away from home his beloved was gained over by his companion, and he to revenge himself seduced the other's wife. They then drew all the members of the ruling class into their quarrel and made a revolution.[7]

Aristotle did not regard force as being essential to the act of revolution. An alternative way, he saw, was the achievement of power by stratagem, force being applied in the name of the reconstituted state.

> Revolutions are effected in two ways, by force and by fraud. Force may be applied either at the time of making the revolution or afterwards. Fraud, again, is of two

kinds; for (one) sometimes the citizens are deceived into
a change of government, and afterwards they are held in
subjection against their will . . . (two) in other cases the
people are persuaded at first and afterwards, by a repetition of the persuasion, their good will and allegiance are
retained.[8]

Aristotle did not devote a great deal of attention to the
results of revolution, and, strictly speaking, did not develop the
theory of the revolutionary dynamic. The only observation
which he makes which could be taken as how he saw a revolution actually taking place, is the following: 'Revolutions break
out when opposite parties, e.g. the rich and the poor, are equally
balanced, and there is little or nothing between them; for, if
either party were manifestly superior, the other would not risk
an attack on them.'[9]

As a recognition of a rational reaction on the part of an in-
tending rebel, this observation could hardly be faulted. But it
does not seem to correspond with observations of the contemporary world. Perception of the balance of advantage in a revolutionary situation may be incorrect. Furthermore superiority
is not only a matter of strength, but also of timing. In fact, in
making this comment it is clear that Aristotle did not intend to
expound a general theory of violence, but only to report particular observations. This is demonstrated by the succeeding
sentences. What he was concerned to show was why the
'virtuous' did not rebel, even though they might be considered
morally to have the best reason to do so. They were, after all,
living in a society which did not correspond to their need. The
answer given is that they are in a minority, and because they are
virtuous they recognize the fact. Interestingly enough, though
the foundations of Aristotle's thought are based on the belief in
the necessity of order in nature, from the highest to the lowest,
it seems that the quality of conforming to this order, which
Aristotle termed 'virtue', did not in itself make one resistant to

the impulse to revolution. Unlike modern political scientists, Aristotle made an ethical distinction between forms of government, and therefore, at least in his own personal preferences, could regard a revolutionary action as being desirable or undesirable according to type. He saw the virtuous man, the good citizen, as being restrained purely by the practical consideration of his inferiority in numbers.

The philosopher did not choose to pursue reflections under this heading, returning to the basic structure of his work: the tripartite classification of states. He proceeds to assess, in the case of each, what sort of revolutionary movements are most probable. There are many pertinent observations here which demonstrate the characteristic strength and vigour of Aristotle in delineating the material of his observations.

> But of all the things which I have mentioned, that which most contributes to the permanence of constitutions is the adaptation of education to the form of government, and yet in our own day this principle is universally neglected. The best laws, though sanctioned by every citizen of the state, will be of no avail unless the young are trained by habit and education in the spirit of the constitution, if the laws are democratical, democratically, or oligarchically if the laws are oligarchical. For there may be a want of self discipline in states as well as individuals. Now, to have been educated in the spirit of the constitution is not to perform the actions in which oligarchs or democrats delight, but those by which the existence of an oligarchy or of a democracy is made possible.[10]

At the end of this discussion, he proceeds to discuss the preservation of various forms of government in terms which have been followed by writers ever since. The élite must obey the law, avoid wrongs, and should, desirably, be restricted in their powers and terms of office. They may divert attention from internal problems by the invention of 'terrors' in the extrasocietal environment. They should at all times avoid disproportionate increases in power, and embezzlement by magistrates, and exercise perennially the quality of self-discipline. Clearly, only the most able men in this sense qualify for the highest offices in the state, and the discussion of these qualifications leads Aristotle to consider the causes of the fall of monarchies and tyrannies.

As antitheses, Aristotle sees the survival of these in very different terms. Royalty he says, survives, in its limitation. Tyranny, however, is strengthened in two contradictory ways: by the extreme use of force, and the moderate exercise of every other form of power. He notes that the tyrant resorts to 'lopping off' the greater among his subjects, avoiding the community, compelling the members of the community to live in public and using informers among them. In addition he may coerce his subjects into poverty in order to give their money to his guards, and please his guards by continually making war. On the other hand, the tyrant should care for the revenue of the state, and maintain dignity, modesty and a show of religious observance.

Even given the greatest care in these last respects, which are necessary to give the tyranny the semblance of traditional monarchy, and hence that quality which today we call 'legitimacy', Aristotle warns the prospective tyrant that tyranny is the shortest lived of all forms of government. The longest known to him in the Greek world, that of Orthagoras and his sons at Sicyon, continued for only a hundred years. 'The reason was that they treated their subjects with moderation, and to a great extent observed the laws; and in various ways gained the favour of the people by the care which they took of them. Cleisthenes, in particular, was respected for his military ability. If report may be believed, he crowned the judge who decided against him in the games . . .'[11]

In conclusion, Aristotle was critical of the Platonic idea of revolution. He noted that Plato had spoken of his natural causes of decay of the forms of government as a 'cycle', but, he observed, he had not illustrated how tyranny in turn decayed, initiating a new cycle of change. Furthermore, he faulted some of Plato's observations; e.g. that oligarchy was particularly prone to divisions. In terms that seem almost modern he criticized Plato's tendency to subsume all causes of revolution under that of poverty. Only impoverished *leaders* tended to rebel, he observed; others who were impoverished did not, though he did not deny the importance of poverty as a cause of discontent. Aristotle was too much of an empiricist to accept any one explanation and he would probably have been prepared to accept that relief from poverty might in some cases have brought equal, if not greater, discontent. It was a question which the ancient Greeks did not attempt to settle.

Aristotle, then, is the true founder of the study of revolution. But what sort of concept did he hold of revolution? It is at this point that one becomes aware, not only of the full precision of his observations, but also of the extent to which they have been blurred by their subsequent treatment.

What Aristotle was discussing in Book v of *The Politics* was not social dissolution (*stasis*) nor, as such, palace revolution, but political change (*metabole*). In his discussion, he postulated that this followed a cyclical pattern among the various types of Greek constitution. But he did not give this cycle a name. It was the historian Polybius who did so, and by doing so, formalized it into the earliest recognizable implication of the quality of 'returning' present in our modern word revolution.

Metabole was translated in Latin as *commutatio* (change). For the Romans it was, in the political context, a new concept. With political violence they were well acquainted. It formed the basis of their Republican social order, and, as A. W. Lintott says: 'a Roman's decisive criterion for the propriety of violence was expediency, provided that the victims did not have their *dignities* infringed'.[12] Desire for revolutionary change, whether political or social, was habitually called by the Romans 'seeking new things' (*novae res*), or similar euphemisms expressing the standpoint of a conservative society.[13] Since the fall of the Republic largely replaced one form of static society with another, the cyclical concept remained essentially Greek. It did not reappear in vital usage until Renaissance times, though the way lay open for it after the translation of Aristotle's *Politics* in 1260 by William of Moerbeke.[14]

One may say, then of Aristotle that he was the first, and in many ways the most important, observer of the process of violent political change.

Secondly, as a philosopher, he established a conceptual framework within which this process could be observed. Though he did not give his cycle the absoluteness later writers did, his role in the formation of the cyclical concept is crucially important. Plato had not completed the cycle; it was left to Aristotle to do so. Since a substantial proportion of his discussion of change is concerned with how to arrest the decay and the overthrow of governments, it is clear that he did not regard the cycle as being closed, and the instances that he gives make it clear that he realized that there were exceptions to the rules which he sought to draw. But the concept, once initiated, had an attractive simplicity which gave it a life of its own.

Thirdly, Aristotle was an observer of the type of social breakdown and dissolution which we have already identified as being the formative factor in primitive concepts of revolution. This breakdown or collapse (*stasis*) he placed in the context of his cycle of political change. Thus to Aristotle the collapse of the social order had a positive significance. It was a stage on the way, a point at which development, rather than decay, was the significant element to be identified by the observer.

This attitude was the most important legacy of the Greek investigation of revolution. It followed directly from the Greek preoccupation with forms of government and their interest in constitutional growth and development. By accepting that forms of government other than monarchy had a right to exist, and indeed were in many ways superior, they accepted that the means by which they were attained had a positive ethical content. If the power of a ruler was limited by violence, then violence had a positive value in that context. The Greeks themselves did not appreciate the startling originality of this viewpoint. Herodotus, for example, attributes to the Persians a debate on the merits of forms of governments on the occasion of Darius' successful *coup d'état* which is purely Greek in sentiment and in content. It would never have occurred to a Persian of the period, any more than to an Egyptian or a Babylonian, that any other form of government than absolute monarchy could exist, and not be contrary to the will of the gods to maintain a unified cosmic order.

Because the Greeks recognized different types of government, therefore, Aristotle was the first thinker to be confronted with the problem of relating types of revolutionary change to the types of government with which they were associated. So, having placed social dissolution in the context of a unified view of political change, he was able to proceed on a scientific basis to place change itself in the context of a greater social pattern. His over-all concept of revolution thus included both change made by force which was real and present, and change brought about by fraudulent means, by which the would-be ruler used possession of the power of the state to establish his position. Recognition of this principle enabled Aristotle to produce a view of revolution applicable not only to movements which succeeded, but also to those which failed in their objective. Their failure, he saw, was not necessarily due to any merit or demerit on their own part, but to the quality of the ruler and the wisdom of his behaviour. Revolutionary change involved a causal chain of some length and complexity, and its failure at any point of weakness could involve transfers of government the consequences of which were not wholly predictable.

Lastly, Aristotle's concept of revolution did allow for the element of causation. The motivation for revolutions he saw as being primarily individual and hence psychological, and only secondarily arising from the psychological orientation of the individual in the social environment. He did not regard it as being governed by impersonal forces inherent in the social order, or being outside the bounds of control of the men who held office within the state. For Aristotle, revolution was a political concept, not a social one; a phenomenon affecting rule and authority within states, and only secondarily the social composition and ordering of rank within that state. These last he considered were significant primarily as factors determining the course of revolutionary movements, rather than the product of a revolutionary movement as such.

Rome and the changing concept

But, as we have seen, Aristotle's view of revolution, and the concept of the cyclical development of political change, did not go down to posterity undistorted. The main reason for this lay in the historical circumstances of the time. Living as he did at the beginning of new monarchy among the Greeks, he was certainly correct in his observation that the ascendancy of the Macedonian monarchy gave rise to the desire, and in many cases the successful attempt, of tyrants to convert their tyrannies into monarchies. What he did not foresee was the long duration of the Hellenistic monarchies, for though the monarchy that Alexander had made almost universal did not survive his death, the successor states to that monarchy did cover most of the known world. In this world, philosophy was a matter of acceptance, and the accepted view of kingship, characteristically, was as the embodiment of the somewhat plain and uninspiring concept of concord. Revolution was unnecessary and even harmful, being at best merely the manifestation of human self-interest. Though the state was no more than the expression of the need for security, change within it endangered its stability. For political change in a world of reborn, but very unstable, monarchies, was a sordid succession of brawls, palace revolutions and political murders.

After 146 BC, the ascendancy of Rome altered the picture once more. The rest of the Mediterranean basin, still organized into petty local monarchies, wavered in its allegiances according to the internal disturbances which marked the later years of the Roman Republic. The observer of Roman institutions, though not himself a Roman citizen, was therefore likely to take very considerable interest in the great turmoils of the times. The rise of the Gracchi, the wars of Marius and Sulla, and the Social War, which put an end to the autonomy of so many of the Italian city states, were events which to rational men demanded some form of explanation. And a state which in the process of such turmoils continued to grow and to expand as did the Roman Republic was something new.

The Greek historian Polybius saw this rise as being the grand theme of his times. He was concerned to show 'by what means, and thanks to what sort of constitution, the Romans subdued the world in less than fifty-three years'.[15] To do so he adopted the Aristotelian concept of a cycle of political change and turned it into something new, simpler and much less exact. True, in one way his exposition was an improvement on the Aristotelian viewpoint. Aristotle's pursuit of classification had led him to divide states according to their approximation to 'pure' forms of government. He did not devote a great deal of time to discussing 'mixed' constitutions, which did not conform exactly to any of his forms. And yet, despite theoretical arguments against them, such forms undoubtedly did exist.

It was a 'mixed' constitution that Polybius considered Rome had unconsciously adopted. The consuls represented the principles of monarchy, the senate that of aristocracy, and the *comitiae* that of democracy.

If the idea of the mixed constitution was explicit in the statements of Aristotle, the exposition of Polybius embodied one significant change. When Aristotle spoke of a mixed constitution, he meant a state so constituted that it embodied a social balance between the people, the nobles and the magistrates. Polybius, instead, spoke of 'powers'. He mistook the form for the substance, and took the powers of each group for the social reality of their respective strengths. He cannot therefore be credited with a true understanding of power, still less, by extension, of the uses of force. This defect was important because Polybius was the author through whom the concept of the cycle of political change, as the over-riding expression of revolution, was transmitted to the Romans. Bearing in mind Aristotle's emphasis on individual will, Polybius' exposition of the cycle of change makes it clear that he is talking about a very different sort of concept.

> Such is the cycle of political revolution [*politeion anakuklosis*], the course appointed by nature in which constitutions change, disappear, and finally return to the point from which they started. Anyone who clearly perceives this may indeed in speaking of the future of any state be wrong in his estimate of the time the process will take, but if his judgment is not tainted by animosity or jealousy, he will very seldom be mistaken as to the stage of growth or decline it has reached, and as to the form into which it will change.[16]

Polybius, then, formalized the concept of cyclical change. The formalization of political theory accorded well with the Roman tradition of law, but it did not provide anything in the way of a practical guide to a Roman lawyer wishing to survive in a polity increasingly given over to the rule of violence. The aloof disgust with which Cicero regarded the conspiracy of Cataline (63 BC) illustrates well the alarming results of the separation of understanding and action. For though Cicero was well acquainted with the works of the Greek philosophers, and understood the theory of the cycle of political revolution, which he described as *commutatio reipublicae* in one of his later works,[17] he was too much of a Roman, and too much imbued with the Roman tradition of political violence, to see clearly where it was leading. His summary execution, as consul, of the leaders of the Catilinarian conspiracy destroyed the very foundations of legal procedure on which he relied. When his own time came to be proscribed, his own actions in the earlier case were a formidable precedent for him to be accorded the same treatment.

Had Cicero been more of a philosopher and less of a lawyer and had he concerned himself with the empirical research of Aristotle and less with his theory, the history of the last years of the Republic might well have been very different. Nor is this merely a question of unhistorical speculation. With the loss of the Greek tradition, and subsequently of Greek itself, Western Europe inherited first and foremost a traditional view of political violence based on history rather than philosophy. But the history on which it was based was that of the Roman authors of the Silver Age.

It was a cynical, brutal history, for Roman authors did not lack for material. Where Catiline had failed others were quicker to learn. Suetonius notes that Julius Caesar was suspected of participation in his earlier attempt 'at revolution [*conspirasse*] in Rome itself'.

> These four had agreed to wait until the New Year, and then attack the Senate House, killing as many senators as convenient. Crassus would then proclaim himself Dictator, and Caesar his Master of Horse; the government would be re-organized to suit their pleasure; Sulla and Autronius would be appointed Consuls.[18]

The fall of the Republic and its replacement by the personal rule of Augustus, seemed to strengthen the case for the Polybian cycle. But violence did not decrease below the Republic's norm under the Empire, whose early years abound in actual accounts of revolutionary movements and the violent overthrow of rulers. As a description of what in modern times has been called a post-revolutionary situation, the description of Tacitus, though biased, could hardly be faulted.

> Opposition did not exist. War or judicial murder had disposed of all men of spirit. Upperclass survivors found that slavish obedience was the way to succeed, both politically and financially. They had profited from the revolution, and so now they liked the security of the existing arrangement better than the dangerous uncertainties of the old regime. Besides the new order was popular in the provinces.[19]

Tacitus was resigned to the empire. Civil war he held to be worse than any autocrat, a judgement common enough among conservatives, but a far cry from the ethical neutrality of the Greek world. Like Suetonius, his writing gives a wealth of information as to the practical operation of political violence. Not only do both writers describe the causes of discontents, the rise of disaffection and the means employed by rulers to detect and eradicate it, but they describe the actual mechanism of rebellion and the very quantities of force employed, with the tactical details necessary to its appreciation.[20] Even with this information at their disposal, later rulers failed to learn the lessons available to them. (In the light of this it may be thought that Cicero has here been too harshly criticized for failing to understand a situation in which much less certain information was available.)

In the new age of the world state there was no getting away from the disadvantages of autocratic rule and the absence of any formal constitutional machinery of succession. Political violence filled a gap which Roman lawyers had not filled. Roman law itself was not to be codified and regulated until in the process of time the Roman monarchy had once again evolved into a stable dynastic form. In the Classical Age writers from Virgil to Seneca typically looked back to a 'golden age' from which all else had been decline. This concept had its political as well as its religious connotations, and both were transmitted to the rising school of Christian apologetics, where they were joined with the political interpretations of an essentially religious message.

Of prime importance in the new order of things was the decision of the Christian to 'opt out' of a political role in opposing the government of the day. In the absence of a formal constitution the real constitution was one of force, and it was for the citizen to act to modify the unchecked role of the Praetorian Guard, and later the legions of the frontier, in making and unmaking emperors. But revolution, because it involves the use of force, was excluded from the range of options open to the Christian. This, they felt, held good, however depraved or decayed the system patently had become.

The habit of passive obedience was well established by the time of the conversion of the emperor to Christianity. The stabilizing effect of a unified state religion is obvious from the historical record. Yet there were those who in the last years of the Roman Empire attributed both its decay, and especially the sack of Rome in 410 AD, to the Christian reluctance to fight.[21]

In Aristotelian terms, there was a considerable measure of truth in this. By the late third century the Christian 'opting out' had reached the point at which it entirely removed the 'middle class' balance weight by which the equilibrium of the Aristotelian state was maintained. That is to say, those people who had an interest in maintaining the state were not prepared to take up arms in its defence. This left it open to the horde of adventurers who assumed the responsibility of ensuring political change, and did so normally by their habitual use of force. In this sense the Christian attitude towards revolution could be said to be responsible for the onset of the Dark Ages. But of course it was not wholly responsible; nor were there not good and sufficient reasons for it. By this time, in any case, Aristotle was out of fashion. The dissolution of Roman culture had reached the point at which the classics of an earlier age were no longer read. In the next chapter, therefore, we shall take up the question of the attitude to revolution found in the medieval world, and the impact upon this attitude of the rediscovery of the classics.

3/The Effects of Obedience

The new synthesis

The paradox of the Dark Ages is that, at one and the same time, they were an age of social dissolution and an age of obedience. The concept of obedience, indeed, regained strength from the very extent and completeness of the dissolution, and in it a completely new synthesis of the concept of revolution emerged.

Christianity emerged as a systematic movement in the Jewish world of the first century AD. The Jewish tradition was one of obedience towards God, but the agents of God had for long been considered to be the prophets rather than the kings. The Jewish kingship was instituted by a prophet, and the rite of anointing, of consecration of the king, conferred on him the essence of the divine. So when the Amalekite came to David to inform him, rightly or wrongly, that he had killed Saul, David recoiled in horror and said, 'How wast thou not afraid to stretch forth thine hand to destroy the Lord's anointed?'[1]

Violence against the king, therefore, was an act of sacrilege. It was sacrilege even for a member of the royal family, as, for example when Athaliah usurped the monarchy of Judah.[2] She in turn was overthrown by force, and so were an increasing number of the rulers of both Israel and Judah towards the end of the period of the monarchy.

The authors of the accounts of these palace revolts assigned the blame for the downfall of rulers, in the main, to their inherent wickedness. Where the burden of guilt was less obvious, as in the secession of Israel itself from the House of David, their position was more ambiguous. Rehoboam, the legitimate successor to the throne, proposed to suppress the revolt by force,

49

but according to the account in 2 Chronicles, 11, did not proceed with his plans on being warned by a prophet that his action would be impious, since it involved fighting against members of his own people.

Violence was not only not forbidden, but even praiseworthy, in certain circumstances when it was directed against people of other tribes. The description of the assassination of Eglon, king of Moab (which takes a vivid relish in the more unpleasant aspects), is specifically represented as being the act of a deliverer of Israel.[3]

Certainly, therefore, according to traditional Jewish views the Roman Empire had no claim on the obedience of Christians. The Christian attitude was influenced in the first instance by St Paul, himself a Roman citizen, and by St Peter who advised his followers to 'fear God, honour the King'.[4] Towards the end of the first century, when the Gospels became available to the faithful, the general precept of obedience was reinforced by the saying of Jesus, that the Christian should not only render unto God the things that were God's but also unto Caesar the things that were Caesar's.[5]

The first obligation, that towards God, posed, however, an inherent conflict in the secular mind with the duty of obedience to the king made explicit in the second. It was therefore very much in the hands of the early Church Fathers, subject to recurrent waves of persecution and indifference, to interpret how in the particular circumstances of the evolution of the late Roman Empire the doctrine of obedience was to be applied. So long as the secular ruler maintained law and order, and did not infringe the freedom of worship, the conflict remained latent. With the conversion of Constantine to Christianity it seemed, indeed, for a time, that the conflict must disappear entirely. But Constantine himself, who as secular ruler called the religious Council of Nicea in AD 325 with a view to ensuring religious conformity throughout his dominions, unintentionally laid the ground for conflict in an age of reduced secular power with the more permanent and lasting authority of the bishops and the Church.

As social dissolution became more advanced the Church felt itself threatened by the combination of pagan indifference and barbarian invasion. In this situation individual interpreters tended to look to secular authority for protection from the barbarian advance in which they thought all civilization would be destroyed. The clearest exposition of this point of view came from St Augustine, who attributed all use of force in government to sin, and reinforced St Ambrose's repudiation of the right of the Christian to rebel.[6] Under St Gregory the Great this was expanded into a positive assertion that even a wicked ruler had the right to demand obedience. But this obedience was silent and passive obedience. The Christian was deprived even of the right to protest, since anarchy was seen as the greatest possible danger. The removal of the right to protest from the Christian left him with no possible means of self-expression in an age in which self-expression meant expression through the use of force.

So there emerged the doctrine of 'the two swords', spiritual and temporal.[7] Under it, revolution as such could not exist. It is arguable that its importance lies not in the fact that, because of political disorder, it remained essentially unchanged down to the time of the Investiture Contest, but that because it remained essentially the same down to that time, the new, medieval political order grew up only in the face of the maximum resistance of the Church. The corrupting influence of this desire for political stability at all cost reached its peak in the encouragement given by the Papacy to Henry II of England to conquer Ireland.

After the fifth century Ireland had for some decades been the only alternative centre of civilization to Constantinople. But the civilization of Ireland in its political essentials was much more akin to the old, pre-Roman state of Gaul and Germany as described, for example, by Tacitus.[8] The medium-powered kings and petty kings who made up the political structure of Ireland under the high king (*Ard Ri*) were frequently in a state of hostility to one another and indeed even to their nominal superiors. Before the compilation of the *Book of Rights* (*c.* AD 900) the law of Ireland, though detailed in respect to the rights and duties of the individual, did not prescribe for the regulation of disputes and the control of political decisions by means other than by force. Though the high kingship regularly passed to the next lawful successor, many of its holders in this period were described in the *Annals of the Four Masters* as 'kings with opposition',[9] while after the death of Brian Boroma at the battle of Clontarf (1014), no further attempt was made to establish a centralized government. The development of a highly sophisticated political order based on the ritual use of force had, therefore, not only been strong enough for long enough to make Ireland the intellectual centre of Europe, but also to enable the Irish militarily to be strong enough to destroy the Danish threat to north-western Europe. In these circumstances the potential of alternative forms of social organization to that proposed by the Church should be obvious enough.

The ritualized use of force, however, was viewed in the Irish context as being a police function, the establishment of order, and not the creation of chaos. So-called wars between lesser kings or between greater kings and lesser ones, were acts of justice, of punishment for infringement of the law relating to property or sacrilege. In the words of Alice Stopford Green:

> The modern fiction of 'tribal states' has led to the fiction of 'tribal wars' in a country assumed to be without any settled rule of national life, or bond between the states. It is clear, however, that in Ireland wars were rare either between lesser or provincial kings: nor were there any wars of revolt of the people against their hereditary rulers.[10]

Palace revolt was regarded with horror and royal families, who were its victims, with distaste.

At approximately the same time political thinkers in the Islamic world were similarly grappling with the problem of the maintenance of the faith in an age of political chaos. As early as the time of Al-Ghazali, they too had to recognize the separation that existed between the holder of effective military force and the divinely appointed imam or caliph. According to Al-Ghazali the caliph was 'he to whom the wielder of force gives his allegiance'.[11] As long as the authority of the caliph was recognized, government was lawful, for the alternative to declaring governments built on brute force to be illegal would be chaos and lawlessness. The rapid rise and fall of Islamic dynasties produced a debate, similar to that which was to take place in Europe a little later, as to the importance of obedience in maintaining the faith. The results of this debate were embodied in the theory of Ibn Khaldun (1332–1406). Basing his work on the history of the Almoravids and Almohads, Ibn Khaldun developed a theory of dynastic succession, which broke new ground, and, but for the collapse of the Arab world before the Turks, could well have led to a new synthesis equal to that of Aristotle.

The basic regulator of political change was seen by him as being the limits of endurance of the dynasty, itself unlikely to survive for more than three generations of fourteen years each. The establishment of political authority in the first generation gave way to autocracy in the second which reached a peak of power in the third before declining and permitting the dynasty to be replaced by another. Ibn Khaldun's work was of permanent importance in his realization, as Rosenthal puts it, of 'the causal interdependence of the several factors of social life in the power-state: economic, military, cultural and religious . . .'[12] Rosenthal, who compares him with Machiavelli, says, 'Machiavelli also recognizes the causality of history and development in cycles. He is influenced by Polybius in his concept of the cyclical change of constitutions. Whether Ibn Khaldun or any other

Muslim author, knew Polybius is, as far as I know, uncertain and indeed doubtful'.[13]

Nor was Ibn Khaldun, in turn, influential, even on other Muslim writers, before the seventeenth century. Before that time, the effect of his views could only have been to reinforce the process that was actually taking place in contemporary Europe. For the transformation of secular government was the doing not of the political philosophers but of practical men, of secular rulers acting on their own authority. The revival of classical learning in the twelfth century, in countering the new assertion of an effective temporal power in England, France and the Empire, in turn forced the recognition of the need for a new reconciliation of the contradictory set of attitudes to political change available to the men of the time.

The contribution of Aquinas

For the concept of revolution, as for the state, this task was performed by St Thomas Aquinas. The point at which the conflict was most marked was over the question of whether it was lawful to kill a tyrant. By this time, of course, the tyrant was almost inevitably a Christian himself, and the precedents from pagan times were therefore by no means appropriate. Thomist doctrine, therefore, rejected Old Testament examples in favour of Apostolic teaching. However St Thomas was less conclusive as to what an individual might do in given circumstances. 'It seems then', he wrote in *On Princely Government*: 'that the remedy against the evils of tyranny lies rather in the hands of public authority than in the private judgement of individuals. In particular, where a community has the right to elect a ruler for itself, it would not be contrary to justice for that community to depose the king whom it has elected, nor to curb his power should he abuse it to play the tyrant.'[14]

The community could do so because, by the fact of tyranny, the king had revoked his oath, and his subjects were therefore freed from obedience towards him. Ideally, Aquinas suggested, the community itself should not take direct action. Instead it should appeal to a higher authority, and if there were no other authority less high, to that of God himself.

The implied restriction on the direct use of force by private individuals was reinforced by the prohibition expressed in the *Summa Theologica*. 'A private individual may not declare war; for he can have recourse to the judgement of a superior to safeguard his rights. Nor has he the right to mobilise the people, which is necessary in war.'[15] Yet later Aquinas concedes that it is in fact right to overthrow a tyrant and even if carried out by a private individual is indeed 'not strictly sedition; except perhaps in the case that it is accompanied by such disorder that the community suffers greater harm from the consequent disturbances than it would from the continuance of the former rule'.[16]

In the *Commentary on the Sentences of Peter Lombard*, Aquinas made this statement:

> . . . whoever possesses himself of power by arms does not truly become lord or master. Therefore it is permissible, when occasion offers, for a person to reject such authority; except in the case that it subsequently became legitimate, either through public consent or through the intervention of higher authority.[17]

This exception is of the very highest importance. As long as there is a possibility of a ruler obtaining legitimacy, or if a ruler, howsoever wicked, should obtain legitimacy through the forms of public consent or otherwise, the individual, in the eyes of Aquinas, would have been in the most grave danger, had he taken up arms against him, of being rejected and condemned to the utmost available in the way of punishment. Intelligent rulers who gained their positions by force, therefore, from this time forward had little or no excuse if they did not realize the paramount importance of acquiring a semblance of legitimacy.

Only if they did not, could it truly be said that it was praise-worthy, or even permissible, to kill them. This was a sanction that Aquinas, in short, resolving the indecision of John of Salisbury,[18] admitted. Yet already in his day there might be no appeal to human authority open. It remained only for it to be clearly seen that the ruler might use his power to compel popular assent to his assumption of power for the realization of the consequences of this dangerous thesis to become manifest.

Since this teaching has remained the standard authority for moral behaviour in Catholic countries to this day, its importance can hardly be overstated. By Renaissance times it was already well established. Furthermore, in reaching back beyond Roman times to the works of Aristotle which had only just recently become available in translation, Aquinas had deprived most of his opponents of the opportunity to produce a logically argued reply. Not only was his teaching consistent with the patristic doctrine and with St Augustine, but it was consistent in a philosophical sense with itself. Moreover, given the division of Europe into a number of reasonably well-established monarchies, and the relative absence of forms of political experiment, the circumstances in which examples could be made available for its repudiation were rare and far between.

Italy and Machiavelli

Yet there was one area of Europe that was already different. As early as the thirteenth century, there were emerging in Italy the city states and principalities that in the following two hundred years were to make it a close approximation to the conditions of the ancient world. Political change in the ancient sense reappeared with the democratic revolt in Rome in 1143. In city after city, princely families built fortresses and towers, constantly on guard against one another and against the people. Once more, changes of power meant changes of alliances, with first the Empire and later France standing in relation to the city states as Persia had to the Greeks.

Within these city states, all forms of government lacked legitimacy. They borrowed it by recognition by Papacy or Empire. Nor were they protected from one another by the sea, as the Greek states had been. The successful leader was one who adjusted quickly to the ways of an amoral society, who forestalled his enemies or who struck back at them without warning. Swift changes of government accompanied by violence were the rule rather than the exception.

For reasons that are still obscure, these changes came to be known by the Italians as *rivoluzioni*. In his interesting notes on the subject, Arthur Hatto suggests two reasons that seem to be of particular importance.[19] It was a society dominated by the imminence of fate, and from the time of Frederick II the prediction of the future had been a major Italian preoccupation. Astrology sought to forecast fateful events by the approaching conjunctions of the planets, the movements of which were designated by the late-Latin coinage *revolutiones*. Thus a word originally of purely astronomical significance became transferred to the seemingly related changes of political regimes. Secondly, though the revolutions of the planets implied in general a return of favourable or unfavourable influences to their original aspect, the revolutions of politics more specifically referred to a sudden reversal of fate: the casting down of the mighty or the elevation of the oppressed. Both meanings coexisted, without doubt, in the word that was subsequently to be borrowed by all European and in our own time many non-European languages.

A long-term movement of fortunes accompanied by sudden, sharp reversals—such was the original concept of our modern word 'revolution'. As yet it was not related to the cyclical concept of the ancients, the *politeion anakuklosis* of Polybius or the *commutatio reipublicae* of Cicero. Italian society did not offer a view of orderly progression from one form of government to another. Its cycles were of a completely different kind. And it was characteristic that the greatest of all studies of this revival of the politics of violence should have concentrated on the role of the individual and emphasized the element of individual fate. This was the work of Niccolò Machiavelli.

The basic principle of the political use of force was set out in *The Prince* in the following words: '. . . those princes can stand alone who have sufficient manpower or money to assemble an army equal to an encounter with any aggressor.' Force, Machiavelli believed, was essential to any political success. Changes in constitutions, and all merely political devices, alienated old supporters by gaining only lukewarm support from new. 'That is why all armed prophets have conquered, and unarmed prophets have come to grief.'

Machiavelli recognized that the prince could guard against a secret conspiracy 'if he avoids being hated or scorned, and keeps the people satisfied'. But he should endeavour, he thought, to maintain sufficient demonstration of his power, through force, and if necessary by a sharp initial display of cruelty, to instil a salutary fear in his subjects; '. . . since some men love as they please but fear when the prince pleases, a wise prince should rely on that which he controls, not on what he cannot control.'[20]

But in *The Prince* Machiavelli is interested in force only from the point of view of the ruler, and he neither develops a new theory of the state, nor a theory of revolution. *The Prince* is essentially, like Aristotle's *Politics*, a practical handbook based on personal observation. For example, those rulers who have lost states, he notes, were either weak in military organization, or failed to keep the allegiance of the people; or, if they kept the allegiance of the people, failed to hold the people and not lose the nobles at the same time. From his experience, Machiavelli had at this stage already illustrated how the prince could build up a strong military organization, and by what means he might win the allegiance of the people, or of the nobles. But his reasons are empirical. He did not follow the example of Marsiglio of Padua[21] and develop a theory which might serve as a counter to the Church's insistence that rebellion arose from sin. Even if he had, it is doubtful whether his work could have greatly gained in renown as a textbook which was practical, however simple.

Marsiglio saw the authority of the secular state as arising from the election of the principal part (rulers) by the body of citizens (legislator), and regarded that executive authority as having a duty to use its powers for the benefit of the whole. If it did not do so, he claimed, it could be removed in the same way. Since he took account both of the number and of the weight of the opinions comprising the majority in the citizen body, he could have gone on from there to develop a full medieval theory of revolution. He was, however, only interested in using this philosophical basis to combat the supreme authority of the Church in secular affairs.

But though Machiavelli's reputation in his lifetime, and to some extent today, rests upon *The Prince*, this work was conceived only as a by-product of his planned master work, the *Discourses on the First Ten Books of Livy*. Since *The Discourses* were not directly influential on other thinkers, the fact that they contained the much more detailed statement of the causes of revolution which is lacking in *The Prince*, tends to go unnoticed. Part of the reason for this lies in the neutral terms in which they are stated. Machiavelli is not a quietist, in the sense that most medieval thinkers were, but the emphasis of all his work is on combating revolution, rather than in promoting it. The objective nature of his descriptions of revolutionary events is unsatisfying to the politically committed, while from the standpoint of the modern political scientist a particular irony resides in the fact that the ten books of Livy on which he chose to comment are just those which modern scholars regard as being legendary.

At the opening of the third book of *The Discourses*, Machiavelli establishes his view of the decay of states. Whether monarchies or republics, he says, they decay and collapse because of a loss of their original goodness. He makes a comparison with the 'ill-humours' that gather daily in the human body, and must be cured lest the whole perish. The return to first principles, however, can be 'either the result of extrinsic accident or of intrinsic prudence'.²² It is not an inevitable process, and it is up to individual statesmen to learn the lessons of history and to apply them to the maintenance of their states.

Machiavelli sees the first danger to the state as lying in the ambitions of individual citizens or rival tyrants. 'A prince cannot live securely in a state so long as those live whom he has deprived of it.'²³ The judicious use of force, then, is essential to the maintenance of the state, and the use of violence against it is something to be expected as a matter of course. But what form is this violence likely to take?

Here Machiavelli is quite specific:

> . . . history teaches us, that many more princes have lost their lives and their states by conspiracies than by open war. But few can venture to make open war upon their sovereign, whilst everyone may engage in conspiracies against him. On the other hand, subjects cannot undertake more perilous and foolhardy enterprises than conspiracies, which are in every respect most difficult and dangerous; and thence it is that, though so often attempted, yet they so rarely attain the desired object.²⁴

From the instances that Machiavelli gives, it is apparent that a conspiracy to him represents both what we should now call political assassination and the *coup d'état* in the broad sense. The first requirement for a conspiracy, according to Machiavelli, is motive. Therefore the prince should take care to avoid acts that might be regarded as wrong or unjust. Even a single man, who does not fear almost inevitable punishment, may have both the audacity and the opportunity to attack the prince. 'I believe it is not uncommon', he writes, 'to find men who form such projects (the mere purpose involving neither danger nor punishment), but few carry them into effect; and of those who do, very few or none escape being killed in the execution of their designs, and therefore but few are willing to incur such certain death.'[25] The second requirement, therefore, is audacity, and for this reason conspiracies properly so-called (involving more than one person) 'have generally been set on foot by the great, or the friends of the prince; and of these, as many have been prompted to it by an excess of benefits as by an excess of wrongs'.[26]

Most conspiracies are discovered at the time of their organization, either by denunciation or by the efforts of the intelligence system of the state. The most reliable defence for the conspirator, therefore, is to communicate his plan to his associates only at the last possible moment. He instances the case of Darius and the successful conspiracy against Smerdis.

Once under way a conspiracy is likely to be endangered principally by alteration in its plans or by want of firmness in its execution. But the dangers are formidable enough, and Machiavelli goes on to point out that they are infinitely compounded when the conspiracy is directed not against one man but against a group. Not only do the increased numbers necessary endanger the security of the project at the point of organization, but in the action itself a constant suspicion must remain as to whether any one of the group is likely to betray the whole. Conspiracy—that is to say *coup d'état* or assassination—is not, therefore, to Machiavelli, a satisfactory way of proceeding against a plural executive.

The aspirant to power should instead direct his plot against the state rather than the individual, aiming, if necessary with the use of violence, to establish a political supremacy within it under circumstances which do not offer a direct challenge to the holders of power and their personal survival. Though the penalties of failure are not necessarily as great, the difficulties are still immense, and therefore the successful plot against the state must employ either 'deceit and cunning' or be carried through with foreign aid.[27] The remedy for the state against such plots is speedy, effective and forcible action. In an interesting epilogue to this *Discourse*, Machiavelli points out that the overthrow of regimes has frequently been carried out wholly without bloodshed, and that those that have been sanguinary and horrible to other observers have been those in which the motive of revenge, rather than ambition, has become paramount.

Machiavelli, therefore, offers a clear analysis of the stages in the development of revolution and the variables involved at each stage, which for precision and coherence goes beyond the work of Aristotle. As his theory of revolution is centred upon individual action and the force of valour and ambition in human affairs, it is not surprising that his statements on the psychological motivation of men in revolutionary situations are numerous and on the whole satisfactory. What is almost completely lacking is any general appreciation of the social background, and the circumstances in which people feel themselves to have been affronted or deprived. One cannot say that the concept of social revolution is wholly lacking in Machiavelli, as many of his instances relate to the decline and fall of the Roman Republic, but both directly and by implication he excludes the consideration of social processes by his insistence of the fact that the only likely centre for political rivalry lies in the political class, or the nobles.

Machiavelli is, therefore, important as a thinker who examines the nature and mechanics of revolutionary action. He is the first in a series of writers on the subject of the *coup d'état*, which in our own time has been represented, among others, by Curzio Malaparte, Feliks Gross and Edward Luttwak.[28] But above all, he is the first writer in modern times to re-establish the Aristotelian concept of revolution as an ethically neutral political phenomenon, and to attempt to examine it from the standpoint both of the challenger and of the challenged. It is this which makes his work particularly interesting, and it is this, with all its faults, that makes it a major turning point in the development of a political concept.

4/The Sense of Rebellion

The secularization of the concept

As in the time of the Greeks, the basic change in the concept of revolution which began with the Reformation resulted from the secularization of a concept previously inextricably associated with divine authority. The separation of the concept of politics from the concept of authority had already begun before the time of Machiavelli. But the Reformation was the period during which the use of secular authority first became general, and this authority was strengthened by the fact that, under Luther, it extended as far as combating the overall power of the Church itself.

Luther himself saw this use of secular power as a temporary emergency, but one based on wider principles. Its purpose was to defend those who were the defenders of true religion, by maintaining a system of law within which they could preach in favour of purified doctrine. Luther taught, therefore, a medieval doctrine of passive resistance to the ruler, the agent appointed by God to punish wrongdoers.[1]

Secular rule, in turn, proved to have its own dangers for the churches dependent on it. In a world of dynastic states, the demise of a ruler was necessarily accompanied by profound changes in the lives of ordinary people. The strict application of the principle *cuius regio eijus religio* within the Empire placed a premium on the conversion of individual rulers, which their subjects were not always willing to admit. It is not at all surprising that Calvin, in more favourable political circumstances, should have gone one stage further than Luther. Having achieved political authority within the state of Geneva, he reinforced the message of obedience with the overwhelming weight of the consciousness of the consequences of opposing the actions of God's elect. The Calvinist state was one in which revolution simply could not exist. But a state that had Calvinists within it, but which was not Calvinist in religion, could not but be called into question. An historical accident brought Calvinism into a prominent opposition role in France and Scotland, and transformed it into an instrument for the justification of revolution.

It was a very orderly justification. The authority of the people, vested in what Calvin called the 'inferior magistrates', was held to be supreme in religious and hence secular matters.[2] Under the leadership of John Knox in Scotland and Theodore Beza in Switzerland, sanction was given to the people to resist a ruler in the name of true religion, provided that their claim to authority was voiced in an orderly manner. From this, it was a short step to the much more extreme, and influential, formulation of the author of the *Vindiciae contra tyrannos*.

The author of the *Vindiciae* is unknown, as it was published under the pseudonym of 'Junius Brutus'—both names celebrated in the history of liberty. It is, however, attributed to Hubert Languet, a friend of Philippe de Mornay, counsellor to Henri IV (1553–1610). It was written by someone who had the French situation specifically in mind, but who was also fully acquainted with the development of events in the incipient Dutch republics. The *Vindiciae* not only advanced a new theory of revolution, but it also was the first in a series of books which advocated actual insurrection and which have been identified by historians as being among the significant causes of specific movements. Its motivation was religious, and the situation it presupposed was the one in which the prince was of one faith and a substantial proportion of his subjects were of another. Or, in other words, the prince was a Catholic, and the subjects were Protestant.

The *Vindiciae* charged that:

> The princes exceed their bounds, not contenting themselves with that authority which the Almighty and all

good God has given them, but seek to usurp that sovereignty, which He hath reserved to himself of all men,
being not content to command the bodies and goods of
their subjects at their pleasure, but assume licence of
themselves to enforce the consciences, which appertains
chiefly to Jesus Christ.[3]

The author was concerned to show that there was a legal
reason why the people could rebel. He found it in the doctrine of
the social contract. In its words:

Now we read of two sorts of covenants at the inaugurating of kings, the first between God, the king, and the
people, that the people might be the people of God. The
second, between the king and the people, that the people
shall obey faithfully, and the king command justly.[4]

Since all rulers were appointed by God, the doctrine
applied even to heathen kings, 'whether they be chosen by lot
or by any other means whatsoever . . . It is God only that in all
ages establishes, and takes away, confirms, and overthrows kings
according to His good pleasure'.[5] If the people obeyed the king
when he commanded things that were contrary to the law of
God, then they made the fault of the king their own transgres-
sion. But he understood that many might reasonably object that
the cure might be worse than the disease. They might fear 'that
a whole people, that beast of many heads, must they run in a
mutinous disorder, to order the business of the commonwealth?
What address or direction is there in an unruly and unbridled
multitude? What counsel or wisdom, to manage the affairs of
state?'
Therefore he accepted the restriction of Calvin.

When we speak of all the people, we understand by that,
only those who hold their authority from the people, to

3

wit, the magistrates, who are inferior to the king, and whom the people have substituted, or established, as it were, consorts in the empire, and with a kind of tribunitial authority, to restrain the encroachments of sovereignty, and to represent the whole body of the people. We understand also, the assembly of the estates, which is nothing else but an epitome, or brief collection of the kingdom, to whom all public affairs have special and absolute reference.[6]

Here then was the author's justification of rebellion. The king, whoever he might be, was in the same position as was Saul, the first king of Israel. 'Briefly, he, whosoever he is, who has received authority from a company, is inferior to that whole company, although he be superior to any of the particular members of it.'[7] If, then, he was delinquent in performing his office the magistrates could act to depose him, and indeed need not even consult the estates beforehand, in case that the king heard of their doings and forestalled them. Moreover, the author seems to say that if the magistrates were not prepared to take action, it was possible for lesser people to do so. But what the author called 'more private men' were not to take up arms against their ruler unless they had signs of 'an extraordinary vocation thereunto', an amusing and typical piece of post-Renaissance realism.[8]

Significantly the author of the *Vindiciae* noted that it was possible, in accordance with the rules he expounded, for parts of a kingdom to detach themselves from an empire. There were a number of examples of depositions of rulers to which he could point, but the first successful application of his doctrine was to take place in another guise. Christian II of Denmark, Eric XIV of Sweden, and Queen Mary of Scotland had all been overthrown by the estates of their realms acting in concert. But the justifications of each had been made in the particular terms of that kingdom, and were not propounded, as were the *Vindiciae*, as rules universally applicable to all states. Thus although the author of the *Vindiciae* most probably had France in mind when he wrote, only eighteen months after the appearance of his book the Act of Abjuration of the Estates General of the United Netherlands, proclaimed on July 26, 1581, embodied its arguments in a precise indictment of Philip II of Spain.

> A prince is constituted by God to be ruler of a people, to defend them from oppression and violence, as the shepherd his sheep; and whereas God did not create the people slaves to their prince, to obey his commands, whether right or wrong, but rather the prince for the sake of the subjects, to love and support them as a father his children, or a shepherd his flock . . . and when he does not behave thus but . . . oppresses them, seeking opportunities to infringe their ancient customs, exacting from them slavish compliance, then he is no longer a prince but a tyrant, and they may not only disallow his authority, but legally proceed to the choice of another prince for their defence.[9]

Modern national revolutions

The Act of Abjuration was the key document of the first national revolution of modern times. It was, however, not called a revolution by those who took part in it, although the actual word had, as we have seen, been in common currency since the late Renaissance. The authors of the revolt were concerned to show that their movement was no 'casual disorder of the mob, but a reasoned movement sanctioned by the wisest and best in the land'.[10] In any case, such was the separation of the Netherlands from the parent territory that the struggle for independence took more the form of an international war than of a revolution in the sense in which many contemporaries would have interpreted it. The implication that the war was a creative act, something whose essential purpose was not to destroy the old, but to create a new order of society was one that was to be of profound significance for later movements. As Harrington put it:

> Where the people are neither in a state of civil govern-
> ment nor in a state of civil war, there the tyranny, the
> oligarchy, or the anarchy cannot stand by any force of
> nature because it is void of any natural foundation, nor
> by any force of arms because it is not able to maintain an
> army, and so it must fall away of itself through the want
> of a foundation or be blown out by some tumult. And in
> this kind of privation the matter or foundation of a good
> orderly government is ready and in being, and there
> wants nothing to the perfection of the same but proper
> superstructures or form.[11]

The concept of revolution as a process of ordering finds expression after expression in the English Civil War, the War of American Independence and ultimately in the early stages of the French Revolution. As time passed justifications of rebellion became more sophisticated, but they were not essentially altered.

There was, however, a hint of what was to come as early as 1649. The English Civil War had been fought in the name of the people, represented by the Parliament, against the king, and to this extent fell within the Calvinist tradition of authority. The execution of the King, though, was a new and radical step. Writing to justify the course of the revolution, John Milton, in *The Tenure of Kings and Magistrates*, defended his case primarily on the medieval grounds that the king was a tyrant, and secondarily that he was prepared to leave it to the magistrates, or 'at least to the uprighter sort of them', to decide this. He then launched into a further justification, based on the grounds that men, being created in God's image, 'naturally were borne free', and concluded:

> It follows lastly, that since the King or Magistrate holds
> his authoritie of the people, both originaly and naturally

for their good in the first place, and not his own, then
may the people as oft as they shall judge it for the best,
either choose him or reject him, retaine him or depose
him though no Tyrant, meerly by the liberty or right of
free born Men, to be govern'd as seems to them best.[12]

Defended though it was with Biblical references, this
thesis still left his readers too uncertain to be generally accepted,
though it did have its reflection in the utopian movements of the
Commonwealth. It was only with the secularization of political
thought that it could be accepted into the concept of revolution,
and even that had to be preceded by reassurance as to the
ultimate consequences.

It is significant, that the word 'revolution' was injected into
common usage in the English language at precisely the moment
that a modern reader would least expect it. The use of the term
by Clarendon to refer to the events of 1660 was entirely Italian.
It referred to the sudden reversal of fate in overthrowing the
Commonwealth, whose rule he even attributed to the 'evil
influence of a malignant star'. Despite its recent acquisition by
sociologists as one of the 'great revolutions', the name Civil War
has stuck to the events of the years 1642–60; the first 'revolution'
to be designated as such by its contemporaries and adherents
was the 'Glorious Revolution' of 1688—an essentially peaceful
affair.

As a concept of ordering *after* violence, Locke looked at the
events which led up to the Revolution of 1688 and sought justification for the prior act of rebellion. When he listed four reasons
for the dissolution of government, he did so to enable people to
ascertain when they might proceed to re-order the state.[13] In
other words such a re-ordering was only permissible if the order
of government had already dissolved.

These causes are so disparate that it is interesting to take a
closer look at them. Three obviously relate to conflict between
the king and the legislature, or, as the author of the *Vindiciae*

would have seen it, between the prince and the magistrates. Government is dissolved when the legislature is altered or the arbitrary will of the prince substituted for it; where its action is impeded by the prince; or when the method of election to the legislature is arbitrarily altered. The first cause is both more general and more absolute, namely when people have been delivered to a foreign power or their prince abandons his charge, thus implicitly abandoning his trust of the people. Governments may also, of course, be dissolved from without by foreign intervention. In all these cases it is lawful for the people to proceed to choose what sort of government they may.

Nearly one hundred years later Thomas Jefferson used all these grounds and more in his indictment against King George III, an indictment which for its masterly drafting and precision has become a classic of its kind. It did not, however, say very much that was new, and it cannot be said that the American Declaration of Independence added anything very important to the concept of revolution as such. What it did do was to add resonance to traditional ideas and to provide a model which others were to copy later. It cannot be said that any of these versions represent an improvement on the original.

The Declaration's significance lies in its opening explanation that it is issued to inform the world as to why the people of the United States are taking such a drastic step as to sever their connection with their former ruler. (The charges themselves, though interesting in their variety, were by that time almost traditional.)[14]

> We hold these truths to be self-evident, that all men are created equal, that they are endowed by their Creator with certain unalienable Rights, that among these are Life, Liberty and the pursuit of Happiness. That to secure these rights, Governments are instituted among Men, deriving their just powers from the consent of the governed, That whenever any Form of Government becomes

destructive of these ends it is the Right of the People to alter or to abolish it, and to institute new government...[15]

Fifty years later, on the eve of his death, Jefferson expressed his final considered opinion on what he hoped the Declaration might have meant for the world.

May it be to the world, what I believe it will be, (to some parts sooner, to others later, but finally to all,) the signal of arousing men to burst the chains, under which monkish ignorance and superstition have persuaded them to bind themselves, and to assume the blessings and security of self-government. The form which we have substituted restores the free right to the unbounded exercise of freedom and opinion. All eyes are opened or opening to the rights of man. The general spread of the light of science has already laid open to every view the power of truth, that the mass of mankind has not been born with saddles on their backs, nor a favoured few, booted and spurred, ready to ride them legitimately, by the grace of God.[16]

How did the Declaration come to have such an astonishing impact? The answer is, of course, that it did not, at least not of itself. What mattered was the sequence of historical events that followed it, culminating in the establishment of the Constitution of the United States in 1787. First and foremost, this sequence dramatized the possibility of reconstituting the social order, once violence had been employed to liberate it from its former rulers. Since the Revolutionary War resulted in the liberation of the 'New World', the men of the revolution acted in the confidence that things could be different; that they were, indeed, inaugurating a 'new order of the ages'.

But what was this new order? The constitution of a republic —a state modelled on the classical features of ancient Rome. At long last, the Aristotelian tradition was joined with the Roman:

not with a Roman concept of a political cycle, for as we have seen, they did not have such a concept, but with the concept of religious cycles (*saeculorum*) planned according to the movement of the planets. The word 'revolution' implied the turning back of the cycle to the aspect of an ideal order.

In this turning was to be discerned the first hint of the nine-teenth- and twentieth-century preoccupation with the inevitability of political change. To it, many men had contributed. Above all, there were Descartes and Newton, whose successive rationalizations of the universe had led thinkers to extend similar hopes to the sphere of social and psychological behaviour. But note should also be made of thinkers such as Locke, LaMettrie, Bayle and Condillac among the students of human behaviour, and the Encyclopaedists among those of social behaviour. By establishing a *secular* (significant word) state, the men of the American Revolution had removed 'the ghost in the machine' for the study of political change, as for its practice.

At the same time, paradoxically, their concept of the meaning of change was highly moral. Change was a means to human self-realization, hence to improvement. But the development of so powerful a concept could not have been achieved but for the previous emergence of a new and more realistic concept of political authority. Harrington had related forms of government to the purely material consideration of the distribution of property within the state. He had outlined his views on the ideal state and had suggested institutional devices for its maintenance, pointing out that the law could be used to change the distribution of property and so to ensure the maintenance of the society. The refinements given by Locke to the concept of property had two divergent effects. In England they led to a conservative reaction and ultimately to the position of Burke in resisting the excesses, as he saw them, of the French Revolution.[17] In the United States, under what Harrington would have called its 'provincial' or, in modern terms, 'colonial' form of government, it was interpreted in the exactly opposite sense. Finally, the development of the concept of the 'general will' by Rousseau removed the need for reliance on the concept of the inferior magistrates.[18] The stage was set for the democratization of the concept of revolution.

France and the democratic concept

To later generations the democratic concept of revolution is inseparably associated with the French Revolution of 1789. Ironically, the importance of this movement to the development of the concept lay precisely in the fact that it came when the concept was already widely accepted. For years before 1789 it had been a matter of general agreement that a revolution of some kind was in the making. What form it was to take, and how significant it might prove to be, lay in the future. But it was certain that it would come.

For this, undoubtedly, the nature and success of the American Revolution must be accounted largely responsible. Not only did France play the role of ally to the infant American republic, but Frenchmen fought in the revolutionary armies and returned home to raise their voices in support of the reforms of 1789. Being soldiers the prospect of violence had no particular terrors for them, though it is unlikely that they saw the revolution as being essentially a violent movement. Rather they considered that the example of the New World would be repeated in the Old in the sweeping away of outmoded social customs, restraints and barriers of all kinds, and their replacement by an orderly society founded on reason. In a very real sense, though, the actual course of the French Revolution came as a shock to many who had been previously sympathetic. As de Tocqueville put it: 'What, to start with, had seemed to European monarchs and statesmen a mere passing phase, a not unusual symptom of a nation's growing pains, was now discovered to be something absolutely new, quite unlike any previous movement, and so widespread, extraordinary, and incalculable as to baffle human understanding.'[19]

The reasons for this bewilderment were not hard to seek. The French Revolution began, as had other revolutions before it, as an essentially political event. It was an attack on 'a vast centralised power', the government of the most powerful and centralized state in Europe. And its purpose, as its contemporaries saw it, was to modernize France and to make it truly worthy of the place which it already held. Such a phenomenon was one on an enormous scale. Its effects were of European magnitude, and indeed de Tocqueville himself was the first to emphasize how the French revolution was a phenomenon common to the whole of Europe, a stage in the decay of feudalism. This view, necessarily of wide-reaching implication for the concept of revolution in general, is represented in our own time by the thesis of the 'European Revolution' propounded by John Lukacs.[20]

Secondly, the revolution, accepted by many as being European in scope, had nevertheless occurred first, not in the most backward states of Europe or the East, but in France. This fact was important in several ways. It suggested to the Saint-Simonians and hence to Marx that revolution was a stage of historical development due to be reached in turn by countries at an advanced stage of industrial growth. It suggested at the same time, to the French revolutionaries themselves that the inevitability of the movement lay in the inefficiency of the old regime which they were dedicated to setting right and replacing by a government more powerful and more effective, reigning in the name of the people. As de Tocqueville commented, 'True, the governments set up were less stable than any of those it overthrew; yet, paradoxically, they were infinitely more powerful.'[21] Thirdly, it suggested to de Tocqueville himself that the reason for the fall of the royal government lay not in its inefficiency but in the degree of hypertrophy which made it resistant to change and unadaptable in the face of change from without. Certainly, the expense of French participation in the War of American Independence had much to do with the bankruptcy of the royal government which brought on the crisis of 1788.

The French Revolution's most permanent contribution to the concept of revolution, however, lay in the glory and dignity that it gave to it. On the one hand, it provided an example of over-whelming success in the destruction of an old government and its replacement by a new and apparently more rational form. On the other, it provided a logical justification for other revolutionaries, whose participants could now simply borrow a new ideology in which revolution became an end in itself and its own justification. In large part this was due to the fact that the revolution took place towards the end of a period in which the ideas of Jean-Jacques Rousseau were venerated in all quarters of literate French society. The concept of the 'general will' was given sharpness and point, firstly by its use, as a basis for the Declaration of the Rights of Man and of the Citizen, secondly by its application in constitutional practice, as in the French constitution of 1791, and thirdly by its polemical use as a defence against the charge of factionalism. All factions of the revolution appealed to Rousseau to justify their actions.[22] But in its most extreme form, under Robespierre, the doctrine was sharpened to exclude from the right to be heard, or even to live as members of the state, all who appeared to be against the proposed revolutionary change of leaders.[23] This was accompanied by the spectacular execution of the heads of the noble families of France, their wives, their children, the king and queen and a whole host of other people of standing within the royal state whose sole crime was to have existed under the pre-revolutionary form of government.

The significance of this lay in the fact that the proponents of the revolution saw it as a finite process. Mankind was essentially perfectible, and this perfectibility was an end in itself which the destruction of the restraints upon man's nature would permit to be achieved in its own good time. Later revolutionaries were to be struck by this aspect of the revolution (where contemporaries might have been more cynical), and to suggest that revolution was, as a means of achieving perfectibility, infinitely superior to any process of peaceful evolution, since at least its results were visible.

The French Revolution in its later stages was a process of construction out of the debris of what had gone before. The royal French government, together with its armed forces and other agents, had collapsed, and revolutionaries were free to reconstruct the social order in whatever way they pleased. They passed laws changing social property relations; they instituted a new calendar; they swept away the Christian religion and attempted to instal one of their own—there was no aspect of social life that was not affected by the political events of 1789–95.[24] Though some of these ideas disappeared as being purely experimental, and others were resisted by conservatives who felt that they had gone too far, a great many of them were embodied in the wholesale revision of French law, the *Code Napoléon*. In consequence, future generations saw the French Revolution almost more as a social process than a political one. The political act of destruction of the royal regime, the transitions of power from one set of rulers to another: these were seen as being mere incidents in a process of social reform of largely autonomous derivation.[25]

Lastly the French Revolution, as a political and social event, gave rise to a long period of world-wide war. Frankly interventionist in the politics of its neighbouring states, and proselytizing with a more than religious fervour, its leaders altered the map of Europe and by removing its anomalies left a clear field for statesmen to establish the pattern of the balance of power of the years after 1815. To later observers, therefore, the French Revolution suggested that revolution was an international phenomenon as well as a merely local one; a phenomenon that not only crossed national boundaries but actually renewed the concept of nationalism itself.[26] Under its shadow the Greek, Serbian and Latin American wars of independence all took place, and the governments of the new countries derived from it the idea of making use of violence to secure their ends, and of establishing the logical pattern of human life for which it stood.

The historical argument about the causes and the consequences of the French Revolution rages on to this day. The force of its example remains. Writing in 1938 the historian Crane Brinton, in one of the first modern comparative studies of revolution (and the one which has probably been the most influential) chose to deal only with revolutions which approximated to the type of the French Revolution.[27] In comparing these—the English, American, French and Russian Revolutions—he derived his terminology from the one with which he was most familiar personally, and with which he knew his readers would be most familiar, namely the French Revolution. Almost contemporaneously, the work of George Sawyer Pettee in its emphasis on the type of the 'great social revolutions', did for sociologists what Brinton did for historians: namely, he fixed a pattern, an ideal type, a standard against which other revolutions should be measured.[28] Not surprisingly, most of them appeared to fall short, and this in itself gave rise to a series of judgements which has forced a radical revision of the concept of revolution in recent years. Before dealing with this, and other problems, however, it will be necessary to consider the contribution of post-1789 thinkers in their own right.

5/The Theory of Inevitability

The idea of social revolution

In 1791 Thomas Paine, who had already achieved fame as the leading pamphleteer of the American Revolution, wrote a short pamphlet in reply to the attack by Burke on what he saw as the excesses of the French Revolution. This pamphlet, entitled *Rights of Man*, concisely stated what was to become the nineteenth-century view of the French Revolution.

> What we formerly called Revolutions, were little more than a change of persons, or an alteration of the local circumstances. They rose and fell like things of course, and had nothing in their existence or their fate that could influence beyond the spot that produced them. But what we now see in the world, from the Revolutions of America and France, are a renovation of the natural order of things, a system of principles as universal as truth and the existence of man, and combining moral with political happiness and national prosperity.[1]

A very different note was struck in 1835 by Giuseppe Mazzini, the Italian nationalist leader, and one of the most celebrated nationalists of the period. 'The French Revolution must be considered, not as a programme, but as a summary', he wrote, 'not as the initiative of a new age, but as the last formula of an expiring age.'[2] In this sentence was posed the nineteenth-century revolutionist's challenge to the orthodoxy of his day, which was to be taken up and given new depth and impetus by Marx and Engels. To understand why, it is necessary to examine the situation as it had become by 1848 and to consider what the established views of revolution were at that time.

As has already been seen the principal, and indeed the only acceptable, model then was the French Revolution of 1789. A process of historical interpretation, subsequently to culminate in the exposition of Alexis de Tocqueville, saw this movement in terms of historical failures; on the part of government a failure to meet grievances of a more or less legitimate character. These expositors saw, too, that this was a movement of a new type, or at least of a new extent, and one with features which distinguished it from all previous movements, and they termed it a social revolution. The causes of this social revolution they saw in sociological terms as social dysfunction.[3] In this they were not in fact original. Aristotle had spoken of the social causes of revolution, and had given guidance to rulers on to how to avoid them. So too had Machiavelli. But the influence that the later thinkers were to have on their successors was more important than the originality of their doctrines. Their influence was largely due to the fact that the most prominent opposition view was a strictly, and rather narrowly, conservative one.

The conservative view saw the French Revolution, like all other revolutions, as the product of dangerous radicalism and the inflamed ambition of individuals.[4] This doctrine, too, was not original. Revolution would have been so regarded by medieval theologians, and in our own time it has been regarded in this way by so-called advocates of the 'conspiracy theory' of history. But its static nature was intellectually and morally unsatisfactory and the effort of the most prominent statesmen in Europe to check revolution by dogmatic conservatism came to an awkward end in 1848 itself with the fall of Metternich.

Meanwhile, for reasons that had little enough to do with politics, people of the nineteenth century had come to accept the theory of human progress, and accepted the concept of social revolution, which had so enlarged their immediate past, as being a necessary part of human advancement. It was, in short, as much a part of progress as the need for women and children to work in the mines, and the barbarities and the cruelties of revolution were seen as embarrassing and unfortunate incidents in an essentially militant process. By contrast, those countries where a purely political concept of revolution was maintained, as in the states of South America, were considered even by their own inhabitants to be in a state of barbarism. One of the most trenchant attacks made upon them, that by the Argentine, Sarmiento, was widely read and influential in neighbouring countries.[5] However it did little enough to check the political process, which Lassalle in 1855 recognized more accurately as an aspect of the 'real' constitution of the nations of that time.[6] In either view, such political revolutions were considered irrelevant to the process of social change, and might indeed act to hinder governments attempting to secure it. They were therefore socially undesirable.

Marx and Engels

Logically, however, the emphasis on the social, rather than the political aspects of revolution, would indicate that the purely political consequences of the French Revolution were themselves undesirable. Indeed so too would be the consequences of any revolution not geared directly to specific social ends. This essentially was the theme of the writers of 1848. Karl Marx and Friedrich Engels became the most distinguished. Being engaged in the process of historical system-building so fashionable in the nineteenth century, they had chosen economics as their basic term of reference and an essentially materialistic foundation for their philosophy. History, as they interpreted it was a history of struggle, not between races, but between classes. The replacement of one system of production with another gave rise to political strains and changes which resulted in revolution. Marx and Engels not only propounded a strictly materialistic interpretation of revolution, but also advanced the startling claim that the historical development which led to revolution was in itself inevitable, and the processes of history therefore would follow certain scientifically determined lines.[7]

The system of Marx and Engels, although much less sophisticated than that of their contemporary Herbert Spencer,[8] had two very important attributes in its favour. It was essentially ✓ optimistic in that it spoke of an improvement in conditions which people might reasonably hope to see achieved in their own lifetimes. The means of effecting this improvement were to be revolutionary. And Marx and Engels based their belief in revolutionary inevitability on the grounds that the processes of historical development (as they saw them) had given rise to the emergence of a new class, the proletariat, whose ultimate mission was to destroy the 'political class', the bourgeoisie, by overthrowing the 'capitalist' state and to establish a new form of government by the proletariat, which, by its nature, would be permanent. The socialist revolution, therefore, would be the ✓ last revolution.

The Marxist view of revolution was first proclaimed to the world in the *Manifesto of the Communist Party* (1848). In it, Marx, with Engels, expounded the economic theory on which his concept of historical development was based. Together they explained to the proletariat the forces that dominated their lives and the reasons why they were summoned to rise against these forces and to destroy them. In concluding with a call to the workers of all countries to 'settle matters' with their own bourgeoisie by revolutionary means they posed, however, a dilemma for their followers that was not immediately apparent. If their concept of the world was right, and the forces that made history were strictly determined, how then did it happen that their book should appear at the moment at which it did, and why was it necessary to tell the proletariat that their hour had now come? The answer, it seems, lay in the lack of awareness of the proletariat, brought on by the appalling nature of their working conditions and their inability to be informed about their circumstances.

It became clear later to Marx that there were others who were no better 'informed' about their circumstances—namely, fellow members of socialist and similar movements everywhere. They might understand the nature of society. They might even accept the Marxist doctrine of inevitability. But in applying these concepts they needed above all greater understanding of the process of revolution. In three great historical works, no less great by having been motivated by propaganda designs, Marx set out to provide studies of contemporary revolutionary movements which would inform those to whom he wished to speak.

He made his first attempt in *The Class Struggles in France, 1848–1850*. From his vantage point in London across the Channel it had, Engels later said, become clear to him that 'the world trade crisis of 1847 had been the true mother of the February and March Revolutions [in France], and that the industrial prosperity, which had been returning gradually since the middle of 1848 and attained full bloom in 1849 and 1850, was the re-vitalizing force of the newly strengthened European reaction'.[9] As a test for this theory, Marx made a prediction: that no new revolution would occur until there was a new economic crisis. In the course of the next two years, however, Marx was forced to make a further deduction, because the destruction of the incipient French Republic by the events described as the 'Eighteenth Brumaire of Louis Bonaparte' was a counter-move that seemed to place the possibility of revolution at the next economic crisis out of court.

Neither Marx nor Engels underestimated the importance of physical power in attaining success in a revolution. 'Let us have no illusions about it', Engels wrote, 'a real victory of insurrection over the military in street fighting, a victory as between two armies, is one of the rarest exceptions.' Accordingly, from the Bonapartist coup Marx drew the deduction that to establish the dictatorship of the proletariat 'one must first of all smash the old military and bureaucratic machine'.[10] A further piece of information was now necessary for the proletariat to succeed in their efforts. But still Marx and Engels did not despair of their task. 'The right to revolution is, after all, the only *really* "historical right", the only right on which all modern states without exception rest . . .', Engels said.[11] It was an interesting conclusion.

It is important to note that Marx did not claim to have originated the theory of revolution as a means of social change. Writing in 1852 to J. Weydemeyer he stated: 'What I did was to prove: 1) that the *existence of classes* is only bound up with *particular historical phases in the development of production;* 2) that the class struggle necessarily leads to the *dictatorship of the proletariat;* 3) that this dictatorship itself only constitutes the transition to the *abolition of all classes* and to a *classless society.* . . .'[12]

Leaving aside the question of whether or not Marx had *proved* anything of the sort, we must be struck by the fact that Marx accepted revolution as a vehicle of political change almost without questioning it. It seems to have been inconceivable to him that change could come in any other way. Nor, despite his historical researches, did he devote any significant amount of time to considering the probable course of his hypothetical social revolution, though he was always quick to point to the errors of others.

It was, therefore, Engels who faced the task of expounding these points with the aid of exegesis from Marx's writings. Apart from the introduction to the histories cited above, the principal statement came in *Anti-Dühring* (1878).[13] Even here, though Engels was insistent on the importance of power to the proletariat, he did not provide them with a blueprint for action, an omission which later Marxists set out to provide for themselves. The results were, not surprisingly, varied, and some were more successful than others. What he did do, following Marx, was to provide rationalization for an essentially obsessive ambition; one which of itself was never subjected to scientific scrutiny.

In retrospect, it must be said that the extraordinary obsession of Marx with revolution was very much a phenomenon of his time. At no period, even during the nineteenth century, were there so many revolutionary movements available for examination and study. It has been estimated that in the small states of Europe in 1848–49 there were no less than fifty.[14] Such a figure has never since been attained. But in the years immediately after 1848 the possibility that the revolutionary movements would subside was not particularly obvious. Marx devoted a great deal of time to the development of movements all over Europe. As a newspaper correspondent he wrote extensively on the progress of events in Spain in the 1860s. In 1870 he was able to watch the experiment of the Paris Commune and to build upon it the last of his three great historical studies, the one that had most impact and meaning for the next generation of Marxists, and for the world at large.[15]

The Paris Commune, the domination of the capital of the world's intellectually most advanced and culturally revered nation, by revolutionaries including representatives of the working class of whom Marx had spoken, was a romantic episode of great propaganda power. In it were fused both nationalist and socialist elements, a tradition of resistance on the part of the French and an aspiration towards something new for other people also. In it were fused also the experiences of 1848 and 1852, of the social-reform movements of the Republic and of the military realism of Bonaparte. It was a drama on a limited stage, a French movement suppressed by a French government, but one acting within the constraints imposed upon it by a Prussian occupation. The birth of unified Germany and the new stabilization of Europe passed almost unnoticed by revolutionary eyes. As Engels said somewhat optimistically 'it was shown once more that in Paris none but a proletarian revolution is any longer possible'. In fact, as later generations have shown, almost every revolution has proved possible except a proletarian one.

Though the *Communards* were by no means all Communists, there were enough Communists among their number to make their destruction a significant blow to the immediate further development of the orthodox Marxist school. The new world, which Marx and Engels had seen as being an arena for revolution, turned out to aspiring revolutionaries to be the very citadel of reaction. The repressive measures of these years, which were, except in 1876, accompanied by almost thirty years of exceptional quiescence in revolutionary events, did play their part in creating the generation of revolutionaries which were to be successful in Russia in 1917. But they did so by interaction. Meanwhile, the stage was held by the proponents of 'the idea'. The flowering of anarchism derived directly from the strength of contemporary states. It preached the destruction of the state by the destruction of its officials. With the ending of the state the people would have a new chance to create society in a new and spontaneous form.[16]

Anarchism; the twentieth century

The spontaneity of anarchism was both its strength and its weakness. The means were within the capacity of any individual with the ability to get hold of a pistol or a bomb. The advance of technology put the raw materials in the hands of many who were unfitted to use them politically, but who lacked the will to live and to build and were prepared to face destruction as martyrs in the cause of 'the idea'. The assassinations of the tsar of Russia, the president of the United States, the empress of Austria, the king of Serbia and a host of others, although they affected the politics of each and every one of those countries profoundly, did not cause more than a tremor in the functioning of the state machine itself.

The insignificance of anarchism at this stage of its development as an active political force is shown by the fewness of its number of martyrs. Apart from the name of Francisco Ferrer in Spain[17] the names of those martyred in the cause of anarchism were in general people associated with only localized incidents, and not with contributions to the theory of anarchism itself.

Their views on revolution are primarily of importance because they contained a rationalization of a phenomenon that had never been wholly eradicated from human society, namely political assassination, and, uniquely, recognized its significance as a consciously revolutionary act. Furthermore, anarchist theory contributed powerfully to the outbreak and development of the Spanish Civil War which in the twentieth century was to be for a fresh generation a formative factor in the creation of a new concept of revolution.[18]

But for the moment the social revolutions that actually came into existence at the beginning of the twentieth century conspicuously owed little or nothing to either the Marxist, or the anarchist, theories of revolution. Characteristically, they took place in economically backward countries such as Morocco, Turkey, Mexico and Iran.[19] They involved a combination of intellectual ferment and of plebeian unrest, the culmination of which was politically effective in securing control of the machinery of government, and inconclusive in the policy which it then set out to pursue. In some sense the unsuccessful Russian revolution of 1905 was of this kind, as was the military vendetta which led to the overthrow of the Serbian dynasty in 1903.

When the proponents of these revolutions turned to theoretical justifications to explain their concept of revolution and what it was about, characteristically they went back to the French Revolution of 1789.[20] Only in the special case of the 'wars of self-determination', of which more will be said later, was much made of the experience of the nineteenth century. These states were states where men felt they had been by-passed by the nineteenth century, where the desire for modernization and creation anew was uppermost, and the old regime was so rotten that no powerful intellectual incentive was needed to support a movement against it. In these circumstances the importance of technique in revolution could be more easily studied. For a European movement, with a powerful intellectual justification, it was clear that the opportunity for making a revolution could be found at a point at which the government of the state was already in disorder. The economic crises foretold by Marx had not provided this opportunity, though that of 1907 may well be considered as in some sense responsible for the developments in Iran and in Mexico. The social dissolution brought about by the impact of the First World War was to prove a much more powerful catalyst.

It was this combination of technique and incentive that made the October Revolution in Russia the most important of the nine successful revolutionary movements of 1917. The ultimate decision to choose the path of the *coup d'état* was taken by Lenin, a successful decision for which the leader of the revolution must be given full credit.[21] The movement, however, was begun by Trotsky and staffed by the former cavalry officer Antonov-Ovseenko. It was their work that ensured the seizure of power in Petrograd overnight, using the peculiar characteristics of their power base—the workers' movements in the capital—to effect the isolation of government by technical, rather than military means. Once in power, it was Lenin's sense of timing and tactics that enabled the highly unstable government, in a country ravaged by war and lacking direction, to create a new state organization which was hailed by supporters and observers alike as being the fulfilment and the proof of the Marxist prediction.

In fact, however, this subsequent interpretation of the revolution in terms of Marxist theory misled opponents and supporters alike. It was not a spontaneous movement by the proletariat, nor even one that was guided and directed from without but carried out by the proletariat. It was a classic piece of civilian/military tactics tailored to a specific occasion and designed to acquire power for a small directing group. Though this had immediate implications in terms of similar movements in other parts of the former Tsarist empire, it is reasonable to say that the Marxist interpretation obscured the real lessons of the revolution to an extent that the carrying out of similar movements in other parts of the world was actually delayed. What Lenin had proved, if anything, was that it was not necessary to have the support of the proletariat in order to make a successful revolution in its name. This was not the concept of revolution which he held, nor was it a concept which, without the justification of success, would have proved immediately attractive to people who were of his way of thinking. The long delayed 'fulfilment' of Marx's prediction, therefore, contained within it the seeds of its own frustration and necessitated within a generation the formation of a new concept based on the experiences of 1917 as well as of 1848.

6/The Attraction of Permanence

Lenin's role and theories

Though the Russian Revolution was of profound significance for the concept of revolution generally, it was mostly so for the contribution of the Marxists. Afterwards it seemed merely a curious historical fact that Marx himself had contributed little to the Marxist concept, and that it might more accurately be called the 'Engels concept'. (Its chief interpreter and most formative contributor was of course neither of them; it was Lenin.)

The reason for this, quite simply, is that Marx never had a real opportunity to analyse a revolutionary event that resulted in the acquisition of power for a group determined to erect the kind of society which he had in mind. The revolutionary events of his lifetime were 'bourgeois' revolutions, though the Paris Commune was reasonably 'proletarian' without, however, being successful. His view of what would happen afterwards, too, was incomplete, for although he had some ideas on the subject, it was not possible for him to back them with specific instances.

Engels, his disciple, was in no better position, though by the fact that he outlived Marx he found it necessary to rebut the views of others, and in doing so unintentionally created many of the most important features of the Marxist view.

The main point which Engels had to establish was that the kind of social change he desired could only take place through the violent destruction of the state. The state was the force of the bourgeoisie, backed by its military and bureaucratic machine. It was 'a special repressive force'. This force could only be destroyed by the seizure of the means of production in the name of the proletariat, and the establishment of the 'dictatorship of the proletariat'. To ensure the eradication of every trace of the state, it would be necessary for the dictatorship of the proletariat to develop its own means of armed suppression. But, when the need for it had died away with the eradication of thel astremnants of bourgeois domination, it would be possible to allow this machine to 'wither away' until there was no trace of it left, and the rule of the proletariat no longer embodiedthe forms of the state.

Clearly, the kind of post-revolutionary society which Engels had in mind was a very different one from any society known at the time. More importantly, it was not the same kind of society as the one that the anarchists envisaged. They foresaw the destruction of the state but believed that when it had disappeared there would be no rule, whether of classes or otherwise, but instead a condition of free and independent association. In this situation human impulses would be regulated only by the individual in the name of the spirit of society. This was not at all what Engels had in mind, since it was this absence of regulation that in his view, and that of Marx, was bound to lead back to competition, and hence the re-ascendance of the selfish element that made up the bourgeoisie.

Even Engels, however, was unspecific about the actual form of government which would succeed the revolution. When in 1917 Lenin found himself in power, it was immediately necessary for him to guide the Soviets—councils of workers and peasants—in making decisions on many urgent matters that had both immediate and long-term social implications. These decisions had not been mapped out in advance. The form that they took was dictated by the existence of the Soviets themselves. As councils, they were similar to those that had been brought into existence at the time of the abortive revolution of 1905, and they were therefore well established. Indeed, such councils and committees are a necessary feature of all revolutionary organization, and they are more important the larger the scale of the revolution. For they form the basis of the alternative system of government that the revolutionaries seek to create.

Though Lenin spoke in the name of the Soviets, he did not

owe his power to them, but to the seizure of the machinery of government so brilliantly organized by Trotsky. Yet this was no simple distinction. Lenin carried the authority for his actions from the existence of the Soviets, and Trotsky himself had emerged into history by the role he had played in the earlier version of the St Petersburg Soviet.

In his pamphlet published in 1917, *State and Revolution*,[1] Lenin advanced a justification of his position. The great bulk of his argument was devoted to demonstrating the correctness of his view that the destruction of the state was vital, and that it could only be achieved by the use of violence. In other words, the pamphlet was first and foremost a justification of the course he had taken in October. It was necessary precisely because the technique he had used was suspect according to strictly orthodox views of the historical predictions made by Marx and Engels.

But in the tradition of Marx himself, Lenin's method of justification was to attack the position of others, preferably one logically unrelated to the position he was defending. So his attack was directed against the so-called 'revisionists' view not of the seizure of power, but of its subsequent use. He heaped abuse on them for believing that the post-revolutionary state would rapidly 'wither away', and particularly on those who had had reasonable doubts about the future of government after the revolution and had thus doubted the efficacy of revolution itself. Lenin pointed to the existence of the Soviets as proof of the 'proletarian' character of his movement. More tellingly, he pointed to the elimination of special privileges for those of his followers who were engaged in the task of government. This in itself, he contended, was sufficient. They must now follow the advice of Engels by exercising the fullest possible control over every aspect of life in Russia.

Lenin's intention was to establish not only that the dictatorship of the proletariat was absolutely essential to the eventual creation of a Communist society, but that it must be a dictatorship. The exploiters of society, he said, must be suppressed by the exploited. Every element of individualism and opportunism must be eradicated. In short, the proletariat must make use of every possible means to establish their rule on a permanent basis, as the necessary precondition to the establishment of a form of society in which they would rule themselves.

The importance of this for the development of the concept of revolution in the twentieth century is obvious. The Russian Revolution was a spectacular event in itself; the dissolution of the former Tsarist empire in the middle of a great war giving rise to secessionist movements which in turn provided impulses for nationalism in other parts of the globe. All revolutionaries are quite naturally attracted by the prospect of establishing their own rule on wholly secure foundations. They have, after all, a good example before them of what is likely to happen to them if they do not. Now Lenin was saying that his method of control was the way to follow; that he could achieve what the French Revolution had not, namely, a post-revolutionary society to which the old rulers would not return. The Marxist (or Engels) concept of revolution was placed in a completed historical context. It was no longer just a means of destroying the old, but a means of creating a new, permanent, ideal society.

The breadth and depth which this gave the concept was such that, even in the long years of Stalin's dictatorship, those (such as Palme Dutt in England[2]) who had believed that the revolution would bring more immediate benefits retained their faith that the Russian way would ensure the ultimate future. Furthermore, this faith made many of them ready to justify almost any action of Stalin's government, however barbaric or ridiculous. They explained the failure to achieve human welfare and human dignity, not as a consequence of the methods employed in the violent seizure of power and the forcible suppression of opposition but as the result of the revival of counter-revolutionary elements within Soviet society.

There was in this some carry-over from the French Revolution and from the nineteenth-century tradition of human development. But it was a more aggressive concept, one which made no concessions to mere sentimentality. The individual was either for it or against it. There was no room for a Talleyrand in the new order, though there was space enough for a multitude of Fouchés. The dichotomy did indeed act to reduce opposition, at least for a time. But the interesting thing is the way in which others looked at the Russian Revolution, and its implacable pursuit of permanence, and immediately drew different, and very much more generalized, lessons from it.

Mussolini and the use of myth

The most important of these from a conceptual standpoint was Mussolini in Italy. He adopted many of the practical lessons of the Russian experience, while at the same time taking it as an ideological foe; a necessary one, for it justified him in adopting the methods of dictatorship.

As a politician, and an instinctive one, he had a feeling for the uses of power described by Machiavelli, and, like him, regarded violence as a normal tool of politics. Learning from Trotsky, he adopted the method of *coup d'état*.[3] But he was operating in a very different sort of society—one which was certainly subject to severe internal strains, but had not yet attained the degree of social and political dissolution imposed on Russia by the war. This dissolution he set out to promote by the formation of private armies and the elimination of prominent opponents. Italian thought had been prepared for the emergence of such prospective ruling groups by the work of Gaetano Mosca and Vilfredo Pareto in describing the tendency for political power to accumulate in the hands of a 'political class' or élite.[4] Pareto, in particular, had gone beyond description to suggest that the long-term continuation of such a monopoly in the hands of one élite would be a prescriptive cause of revolution—the violent displacement of the ruling élite by a rival. Such a sense of foreboding was entirely helpful to Mussolini.

But Mussolini's refinement of revolutionary technique owed

most to the work of the French syndicalist Sorel. In his book *Reflections on Violence* (1908) Sorel considered the prevailing pessimism of society and speculated on the reasons that had prevented socialist movements from achieving power.[5] If Marx was right, and their sole function was to oppose the state, why had they not done so? Why, furthermore, had they allowed themselves to be drawn into government? There was a real danger now that when revolution came it would be one with a conservative cast.

The reason lay in the visible failure of the means that had originally been recommended. After 1870 no one could believe in the success of volunteer armies and volunteer generals, nor in the intentions of self-styled representatives of the people. And for a successful revolution to occur, its forces must rally behind a formula for success. This formula need, however, not be 'real'. That is to say, the leaders of the revolution did not have to believe it, though their followers did. Belief in the *myth* of revolutionary success was the *sine qua non* of that success.

Sorel justified his belief in the importance of the myth by reference to the social psychologist, Gustave Le Bon. Le Bon, he said, was correct in saying in *Psychologie des Foules* (1895) 'that the belief in the revolutionary instincts of crowds is a very great mistake, that their tendencies are conservative, that the whole power of socialism lies in the rather muddled state of mind of the middle class'.[6] The opportunity was open to create a new myth of the class war, and to hold out to the crowd the prospect of achieving power through the universal proletarian strike. It did not, finally, matter whether or not the strike would in fact achieve its purported end. The myth would serve well enough as a rallying point for other forms of successful action.

Sorel's own belief in the strike went almost unheeded, though in our own time governments have been brought down by the power of the general strike alone, notably in Costa Rica and El Salvador.[7] But the idea of consciously manipulating the public mind to create a myth of a revolutionary movement which would hasten its triumph—that was the aspect which struck Mussolini. His 'March on Rome' in 1922 was a veritable master-piece of illusion. For one thing, no one marched, and the leader himself arrived comfortably by train in a sleeping car. But the illusion was none the less effective for having been carefully worked out.

Curzio Malaparte, the most important interpreter of the events of this revolution, was fully conscious of its origins and its parallels with the Russian experience.[8] He, as a newspaper-man, was among those who made use of the techniques of com-munication and its control to create that sense of overwhelming power which persuaded the Italian government to capitulate and the king, isolated in his capital, to accept Mussolini and call upon him to form a new government. Where Trotsky had merely sought to isolate the Kerensky government, to render it helpless, Mussolini actively sought to manipulate. In doing so, he achieved power with the full forms of legitimacy, and by seizing control of the state by implied rather than visible force was en-abled to use its full power to reshape society in the way he wanted. In doing so, too, the control of communication was fundamental to his success.

Where Mussolini had led, others were rapidly to follow. The post-war period was marked by a series of intermittent coups in Central Europe and the Balkans. Many of these new regimes adopted a quasi-Fascist programme. All were nationalist, and all sought in a concept of authority the essential guiding prin-ciple for the remoulding of their respective societies. For this type of authority to be fully accepted the myth of revolution as carry-ing its own brand of authority had first to be generated and accep-ted. Techniques of police control common to both Communist and anti-Communist regimes were used to ensure conformity and to impress on possible deviants the utter impossibility of standing in the way of 'history'.

Latin America

After 1930 the end of prosperity extended this phenomenon to a world stage. In Latin America some of the oldest
and best established political systems gave way to the new order.
Argentina and Brazil followed Chile in adopting a military and
nationalist style through violent political change. They were
aided by the survival among their neighbours of the ancient
concept of Caesarism: authority vested in a single leader expressing the will of the people by virtue of his designation by the
military as the custodian of national liberty and welfare.[9] There
was, too, an upsurge of political parties and of various ideologies
designating themselves 'revolutionary' in the vain search for
popular support.

Among these, one stood out because of its success in winning
and maintaining political power. This was the party directed by
Lázaro Cárdenas in Mexico, initially known as 'The Party of
the National Revolution'. He created it in the sense that he gave
it an ideological base in a definable political programme, though
he had in fact inherited both the party and the name from the
age of Caesarism that had preceded him. In the ideology of the
revolution, the element of myth in the success of the revolution's
goals and its implied permanence, was wedded to the concept of
revolution as a programmatic reordering of society. It was
largely indigenous. Though Marxist jargon was popular with
the intellectuals, and Fascist ritual with the politicians, the
Mexican blend, like other less successful nationalist movements,
did not lend itself to export, though it did have its imitators in
Peru and its experience was later borrowed by the Cubans.[10]

That it was successful was largely due to the fact that Cárdenas
himself accorded to the popular will a degree of respect that it
had seldom received anywhere, and certainly not in Latin
America. It was a personal rapport, and was certainly no artifi-
cial creation. But its reality proved the best of all foundations
for the myth. In fact, as politicians in non-revolutionary societies have since discovered, conscious creation of a non-valid

myth is one of the surest pathways to disaster in the event of a change in political circumstances in the outside world. With the acceleration of communication such changes have since become increasingly probable.

The institutionalization of the Mexican Revolution, however, came late. The revolution itself began with a period of violence from 1910 to 1920 which destroyed rather than created. It bore no strong ideological stamp. The 1920s were years of political competition and the gradual erosion of military dominance. In the pattern of the French Revolution (to which ideologically the early revolutionaries owed most) it passed through a stage of corruption and decay before the development of ideologically committed government and nationalist self-assertion. Institutionalization meant reversion to a more traditional style of government, increased central authority and the rest.[11] And yet there were important differences, and one was that the concept of revolution had now been extended to cover periods of peaceful reform unmarked by violence; not a return of the wheel of change or a series of sudden upheavals, but ordering and social engineering. The resemblance to the politics of the New Deal in the United States is indeed striking.

Armies and revolution

But if there is a resemblance between the rise of Cárdenas and the rise of Roosevelt, there is also a coincidence between the rise of either and the rise of Hitler in 1933. In the Nazi case, the techniques of Mussolini were expanded and developed, the creation of a myth of nationalism, and of this nationalism reaching new and extravagant heights. The myth, however, was underpinned by carefully selected and real achievements designed to provide 'proof' of revolutionary permanence. Most important of all, Hitler took heed of the role of militarism in the right-wing coups of his time, and established a dual system of control of the armed forces which was in many respects unique.[12]

Writing in 1943 Katherine Chorley, in *Armies and the Art of*

4

Revolution, blazed the trail for the numerous studies of the role of the military in politics that have appeared since. In particular, she was the first detached and impartial observer to examine their role in revolutionary events. She was critical of the preparation done by revolutionary politicians of the past, and in particular of the socialists:

> Practical revolutionary leaders, with the exception perhaps of the Russians, seem to have attacked their problems *ad hoc* with little reference either to theory or to the experience of the past. In particular, beyond occasional references of socialist thinkers or of long-headed politicians, generally of the Right, whose job has forced them up against dealing with revolution in action, little serious attention has been given to an effort to make an historical analysis of armed insurrection in its relation to the character and strengths of the defending force of the *status quo* government which the insurrection is designed to overthrow.[13]

Katherine Chorley, recognizing that the ideological differences of revolutionaries did not necessarily imply similar differences in their techniques for seizing power, returned to the old concept of revolution as covering all forms of violent political change. She was well rewarded. Primary consideration of revolutionary events led to the enunciation of the essential function of the role of the military, which, although known to many generations as a rule of thumb, had not previously been submitted to a general systematic analysis. 'The rule . . . emerges clearly,' she wrote, 'that governments of the *status quo* which are in full control of their armed forces and are in a position to use them to full effect have a decisive superiority which no rebel force can hope to overcome.' Revolutions, therefore, might particularly be expected in 'the last stages of an unsuccessful war'.[14] Illustrating her remarks by reference to the actions of

Thiers in combating the Paris Commune, she pointed to the importance of withdrawing the army from possible political contamination and restructuring it before embarking on direct suppression of revolutionary movements. It is interesting to note that in the more specifically military aspects of the book, many important deductions were made by her from the experience of Ireland, significant as the only territory successful in seceding from a victor of the First World War. For Ireland's important role in the politics of the League of Nations and in the development of the British Commonwealth marked, perhaps, the high point in the acceptance of revolution as a 'respectable' act.

Ireland's experience, though significant, was so individual that even the word 'revolution' was seldom heard there. In the ideology of its leaders, which was almost wholly pragmatic, there was little or no echo of outside controversies. Its socialist element was negligible, though in recent years the rise of the Irish Labour Party has led to some desultory reappreciation of the role of James Connolly as one of the leaders of the unsuccessful Rising of 1916.[15] Nor, despite some agitation, did it succumb to the temptation of choosing a Fascist-style successor government. Its native, quasi-populistic programme of social welfare and limited intervention owed much to the support of the Catholic Church, and foreshadowed (but did not much influence) the development of 'revolutionary' ideologies in the Church of the age of the Second Vatican Council.[16]

Revolution and self-determination

Ireland's significance lies in its having waged the earliest, and, as we have seen, one of the most successful, of the twentieth-century 'wars of liberation', or of 'national self-determination'. The significance of these wars, in turn, lies precisely in the fact that they have been so rare. Since 1900, in fact, only fourteen nations have achieved independence by force, compared with over sixty that have done so by peaceful means.[17]

The separation of the concept of 'national self-determination' from that of 'revolution' is in one sense very old. The two were interlinked in Holland, the United States, French Revolutionary Europe and in Latin America. They subsequently began to diverge, partly because of the need for unification rather than secession in Italy and Germany, and partly because of the growing emphasis on revolution as a social rather than a military phenomenon. In 1860 the separation of the independence movement in Italy from the revolutions of the Italian states became patent. Pragmatism, not idealism, achieved the goal of unification there; and in Germany it was 'blood and iron'.

Neither movement, however, would have taken the form that it did had it not been for the concept of the state propagated by Hegel and his school. In a form of secularized medievalism. this concept left no room for the failure of government, still less for the acceptability of its displacement.[18] Though Hegelian doctrines were reinterpreted towards the end of the nineteenth century to admit the acceptability of liberalism,[19] it was only with the destruction of the Central Powers in 1918 that their governments were displaced, and then by the idealism of President Wilson. Referring back to Franklin, Jefferson, Madison and other leaders of the American Revolution, Wilson maintained that the 'right of self-determination' was fundamental—in a situation in which this 'right' was inevitably interpreted in the spirit of a rather narrow-minded parochial nationalism.[20] In consequence, the concept of self-determination rapidly moved away from political idealism in the direction of social realism, and thus, after 1945, came into conflict with the fact that for the great majority of human societies the concept of nationalism was essentially one held by the élite. Mobilization for war demanded something more. So wars of national self-determination came once again to be associated with 'revolutionary' aims: the reshaping of society, the creation of a self-consciousness in society, and, hence, the integration of that society by the political education of the mass of its population.

It was, therefore, one thing to develop the concept of self-determination; it was quite another to apply it. In an attractive simplification the two aspects of the programme—internal social change and external warfare—could be subsumed under the common concept of 'liberation'. The problem was, however, that although the presence of an external foe could strengthen the hand of a revolutionary élite in dealing with internal political opposition, that foe could neither be too strong—for in that event it could suppress the élite and destroy its preparations for revolt—nor too weak, for then it might strategically withdraw from the scene, leaving the élite to run headlong into the opposition generated by its own actions. It was a difficult and perhaps insoluble dilemma when made a matter of practical politics, and one which was solved only partially, by a wedding of ideology and technique whose validity has yet to be demonstrated as conclusive.

Briefly, there were three sets of circumstances in which self-determination might be attempted. Firstly, and most obviously, there was the secession of an isolated province or possession. Here, after a declaration of independence, the territory fought essentially in a state of 'international' war, as in the case of Holland, the United States, Mexico, Argentina, Paraguay and others. In our own time Indo-China, Algeria, Rhodesia and Indonesia followed this pattern with success.

But the empires of Central Europe had by 1918 been consolidated to the extent that secessionist territories were unified with, or at least contiguous to, the metropolitan country from which they sought independence. If they were very small—the second special case—such territories could seek independence by *coup d'état*, as in the case of Vilna and Fiume.

But such a method was only possible in larger territories when the metroplitan country had lost control of its armed forces. For when it retained such control, and had good lines of communication, it was normally able to reconquer its lost province, (the experience of the Soviet Union in Finland being for several reasons ambiguous). Even Ireland's experience had features of this kind, owing to the British command of sea power, while Spain (under French occupation), Poland (under Russian occupation), and France itself (under German occupation), were testing grounds of particular significance. The problem was to attain the element of isolation present in the first category, or the element of surprise present in the second, and to combine either or both to this third, large residual group.

A new form of revolutionary strategy had to be adopted. Secession was already difficult enough, in view of the limited objectives of any secessionist movement. By restricting its goals to separatism, the secessionist movement foregoes its best chance, the destruction of the centre of political power in the metropolitan state.[21] Furthermore, in displacing external rule, it must develop a pre-formed government ready to step into its place, while being under constant and remorseless attack.

Guerrilla warfare

Such a new revolutionary strategy lay ready to hand in the widespread, though badly documented, tradition of guerrilla warfare.

Guerrilla warfare is a strategy born not out of strength but out of desperation. The word itself emerged during the Spanish War of Independence in 1808 to designate small groups who fought in sudden sharp engagements, falling on small bands of regular troops by surprise and defeating them in close fighting. Equally important, once the engagement was over, the group withdrew to rough country, taking advantage of the terrain and its own superior knowledge of it, to outwit pursuit by regular reinforcements. It combined the desirable elements of surprise and isolation. But from the revolutionary standpoint it had serious disadvantages. In the absence of efficient and reliable modern communications (something not readily available to guerrillas even today) it was difficult for such bands to combine to formulate a large strategy, and this meant that they were basically at a disadvantage in forming a future successor government. In the Spanish case, and the partisan warfare of the Second World War, this was not a task that they had to perform, since their allegiance was to a government which had its seat outside the fighting zone in which they operated. Furthermore, they enjoyed the general support of the population, which is something that an internal revolutionary movement of small groups has to create for itself.

As a technique, guerrilla warfare was generally dormant during the nineteenth century. It was absorbed directly into the experience of the Latin American states, but at that period these states had such weak central governments that the distinction between guerrilla and conventional warfare hardly existed. Revolutionaries in most instances sought to further their cause by seizing the grand prize: control of the whole state. The main instance in which it was employed was in China. There the concept had originated separately, and had, indeed, existed for more than two thousand years. It was thus ready to appear again in the 1920s, when the failure of the Republic to form a strong central government was already patent, and the country had relapsed into a loose collection of provinces led by war-lords. Then in 1932 the Japanese invaded Manchuria. Guerrilla warfare offered itself as a natural method of resistance to the well-armed Japanese forces. What gave it particular significance was its adoption by Mao Tse-tung and the Chinese Communists, who had already been forced to retreat to a suitable stronghold in the distant western province of Yenan.

From his practical experience Mao distilled advice on the conduct of guerrilla operations. He was conscious of the value of his base, and no less so of the importance to his movement of educating the local inhabitants to support his movement when it operated outside it. The equality demanded of men operating in small groups against a powerful enemy, he saw, was entirely communist in spirit. But they had to find their support, not among the urban workers of traditional Marxist doctrine, but among the overwhelming majority of Chinese peasants. The peasants were potential friends. What they lacked, in Mao's view, was no more than political education. So with due respect to peasant beliefs and customs, his men set out to provide this as a necessary and equal part of their duties.[22]

It was Mao who fused the technique of guerrilla warfare to the ideology of Marxism. In doing so, he brought about a fundamental change in the character of Marxist thought, one that made it potentially far more attractive to revolutionaries in the colonial and under-developed world. But he did not just give them a doctrine, he gave them a textbook. His *Guerrilla Warfare* with its detailed instructions on the welfare of the peasantry and the organization of guerrilla regiments and formations, embodied a wealth of military experience, and his eventual success in 1949 gave prestige to the technique which had already by then begun to change the outside world.[23]

Directly derivative from the Chinese experience are the military texts of the Vietnamese. Among these may be singled out Truong Chinh's *The August Revolution* and *The Resistance Will Win*, and Vo Nguyen Giap's *People's War, People's Army*.[24] Mention should also be made of the writings of Ho Chi Minh, the Vietnamese leader, for their important ideological content.[25]

As in all revolutionary movements, the important thing about the Chinese experience was its success. For the first time a Communist regime had achieved power though an admittedly 'revolutionary' means which was different from that employed in Russia. It was not orthodox Marxism, but, then, neither was Lenin's *coup d'état*! Owing to the failure of Stalin to support the nascent Communist movement in 1927 against his protégé Chiang Kai-shek, moreover, Mao was inclined, and after 1953 in a position, to claim the role of Lenin's successor as the most authoritative interpreter of Communist orthodoxy. Significantly, before his death Stalin had already authorized the series of revolts in the South–East Asia which led to the protracted 'Emergency' in Malaya and strengthened the position of the

Communists in Indonesia at a time when they critically needed it. From these and other instances no important ideological contribution resulted, though the non-Communist leader of the war against the Dutch in Indonesia, General Nasution, did produce a textbook for his forces.[26] The gain in experience fell to the observers of the colonial powers, resulting in a wave of books on the subject of guerrilla tactics in the early 1960s.[27]

The tradition of guerrilla warfare had, however, never died out outside China. It was employed by the revolutionaries of 1899, as later by the Hukbalahap, in the Philippines against the Americans; by the Afrikaaners against the British, and by the Cubans under José Martí, the poet-patriot, against the Spanish.[28] The chief gainers by this experience were the British, who adopted the technique of 'concentration' of the civilian population (pioneered in Cuba) as a technique to remove the civilian population from their vulnerable position under pressure from irregular forces. It was later employed with striking success in Malaya, joined with the concept of constitutional advance towards self-government used by the Americans in the Philippines. Even in Britain, however, respect for guerrilla warfare remained, particularly since one of the classics on the subject is still the literary record of T. E. Lawrence's irregular campaign in Arabia, *The Seven Pillars of Wisdom*.[29] Here the Arab tradition of desert warfare passed naturally into the concept of the liberation of nations by guerrilla means. And it is in this tradition, rather than that of either Spain or China, in which Frantz Fanon wrote *Les damnés de la Terre* (translated as *The Wretched of the Earth*).[30]

Reference has already been made to the special place of the Spanish Civil War in the development of the twentieth-century concept of revolution. The war itself, of course, can either be regarded as a successful *coup d'état*, or as a very rare example of a case in which an established government was overthrown by its own forces after a long period of conventional warfare. Either way, its interpretation was confused by the fact that those holding 'revolutionary' ideologies were fighting on the side of the government. The immediate lesson which they drew from that experience, and which in any case was congenial to them, was that conventional warfare was essentially 'counter-revolution-ary'. Feelings were, however, ambivalent as to what was to be done about it, and the various 'peace' movements of the late 1930s were in any case soon overwhelmed by the outbreak of global war. There was left a powerful literature glorifying the participants, and a number of well-trained political agents who sought to apply its lessons between 1945 and 1955 in various parts of the world, with varying degrees of success, according to their interpretation of them.

By the late 1950s, therefore, the concept of revolution had in all traditions come to attach special significance to the technique of guerrilla warfare. The idea of mass political education, which formed its basis, thus added a new dimension to the view of revolution as a mass rather than an élite occupation. This was true not only of Marxists, but also of non-Marxists. Consciously or unconsciously, the idea of suddenness, of reversal of the classic concept was yielding to an insistence on protracted fighting and long-drawn-out social change. With the effect on Western thought we shall deal in the next chapter. Here it is sufficient to note that the convergence of views on the concept of revolution led to a generalization of experience, which, though associated with Marxism in particular, had a world-wide significance. Most important among the consequences was the development of the concept of permanence.

Mao's formulation and youth movements

Permanence in relation to the older revolutions and the growth of totalitarianism in Europe had received its formulation from Sigmund Neumann in 1942.[31] It was, Neumann saw, a major preoccupation of post-revolutionary governments. What was significant, he pointed out, was that such governments had now come to realize the potential that lay in methods of social control, and that the control of communication was the foremost factor in enabling them to attach the idea of permanence to the revolutionary myth.

Permanence in the new revolutions, however, received its formulation from Mao Tse-tung himself. Mao accepted implicitly Lenin's interpretation of the significance of the dictatorship of the proletariat, even though the proletariat for him was the peasantry rather than the urban workers. But after 1950, and particularly after the failure of the 'Great Leap Forward' in 1957, he became more critical of the elements of Lenin's postrevolutionary programme. To him, Russia in the age of Khrushchev and coexistence was clearly no longer a revolutionary society. What had gone wrong? The answer lay in the disappearance, along with the period of struggle, of the revolutionary zeal that had accompanied it. To recreate the zeal, logically, he must recreate the struggle. His technique was to make use of the youth who had grown up under his regime and who accepted it uncritically. Formed into the celebrated 'Red Guards' they were sent into the factories, and out into the country, to 'struggle' for the minds of the people. Their very numbers suggested veiled menace to the potential deviant; their vigour in ceaseless argument destroyed the logical foundations of his resistance and supplied new ones for conformity. It is important to note that in the process physical violence was not necessarily intended, though it did occur widely and resulted in the deaths of many of China's scarce teachers. The cost in terms of economic dislocation was high, also, for once loosed the Red Guards proved singularly difficult to control, a task that was eventually performed by the army. How far the creation of the new permanence was successful it is not yet possible to say. It is even possible that it may have resulted in the frustration of Mao's most important contribution to revolutionary theory: the fact that the peasantry need not be an essentially conservative force.[32]

Certainly, however, it had a profound significance for the

emergence of the world-wide 'youth revolution'. Though no country has failed to show the effects of this in some degree,[33] the most spectacular manifestations, and politically the most interesting, have occurred in the United States. That this is so is in some small part due in turn to the appearance of a youthful, Communist regime in Cuba in 1959. This brought together three strands of conceptual development.

Firstly, it coincided with the emergence into independence of all but a handful of territories of the former colonial empires. Since colonialism was no longer a significant enemy, orthodox Marxism, which had progressed from opposition to capitalism to opposition to imperialism, now had to discover a new economic rationalization for fear of its political enemies. This was 'neo-colonialism', the retention of aspects of political control over territories by means of economic ties.[34] Significantly, in so far as it had any factual content, it was a phenomenon common to all developed countries, and was indeed common to the policies both of the United States and of the Soviet Union. Revolution was 'against' neo-colonialism.

Secondly, the accession to power of Castro's Cuban regime occurred as the consequence of guerrilla warfare, of an indigenous Latin American type. In view of the proximity to the United States and the presence of large American economic interests there, many observers jumped erroneously to the conclusion that the United States had aided the old regime, when in point of fact the United States government did not respond with hostility until after Castro was seated in power. It seemed therefore that guerrilla warfare was a virtually 'magic' technique, which could ensure victory in the most unpromising circumstances. This impression was powerfully reinforced by the publication in 1961 of Che Guevara's *La Guerra de Guerrillas*, a text book of revolutionary skills which was not only well written but infectious in its optimism.[35]

Thirdly, not only were the leaders of the Cuban revolution young in an age dominated by old (and often sick) men, but once in power they acted with great fervour to turn Cuba into a Communist state. Visibly they failed to achieve their dynamic economic objectives. Equally visibly they gave Cuban workers and peasants equality and hence dignity. In all of this, youth played an important role, notably in the teams that went out during the literacy campaign of 1961 attempting to teach every Cuban how to read. Most importantly, failure in any respect (and many of the most spectacular Cuban blunders, of which there were a great number, occurred out of sheer ignorance or haste) could always be attributed to the remorseless hostility of the United States.

The idealized way of life

By this time the significance of the word 'revolution' was already so wide that almost anything might have happened to it. What did happen, however, was its elevation from being a specific concept concerned with political events and goals, to an unspecific concept representing an idealized way of life. All the older meanings, of course, continued to be valid in their specific contexts. The idea of violence, unpredictability, the overthrow of the powerful, resistance to domination, and independence remained. But in the new synthesis revolution was much more. It was youth defying age, liberation from the population explosion and social constraints, achieving the impossible, a formula for re-shaping the world in any image, internal or external. The consequences were spectacular, and they are likely to become more so.

Consciously the Cuban leaders aspired to nothing less than the ideological leadership of the 'Third World'. The Cuban experience, they asserted, foreshadowed the path of liberation from both political and economic constraints. The method of struggle lay at hand; guerrilla warfare. Simultaneously, a young French philosopher, Régis Debray in ¿ *Revolución en la revolución* ? (1967) generalized Guevara's textbook into a doctrine of the revolutionary *foco*.[36] A small group of men, he asserted, could form the basis for a socialist revolution through guerrilla warfare. As he

wrote, with Cuban aid, expeditions were attempting to provide
such nuclei in the Congo (Brazzaville) and Bolivia. The doctrine
was attractive. It was economical. It was theoretically applicable almost anywhere, including the urban 'ghettos' and even
the universities of the economically 'advanced' nations.[37] And
—it was psychologically satisfying to believe that small nations
could defy and defeat the large by their own efforts.

But the failure of the doctrine came in its application. The
Bolivian team, led by Guevara himself, was attempting nothing
less than revolution for the whole of South America. Instead,
the team was hunted down and wiped out by Bolivian forces
employing modern tactics of rapid movement (including heli-
copters), tactics which had been by then subject to intense prov-
ing in Viet Nam. The Cuban command, who regarded both
Bolivia and Viet Nam as being 'sacrifices' for the liberation of
their respective continents, was perhaps not altogether surprised.
But the death of Guevara himself, at the early age of 39, provided the revolutionary cause with a martyr, an image which
the romantic circumstances of his heroic death, after betrayal
by those whom he had most trusted, powerfully reinforced.[38]
He was a very real figure whom youth, both in the United
States and in Europe, venerated in contrast to the shadowy
figures of radio, television and the screen on whom they had
been brought up.

The conflict in Viet Nam was so ambiguous that it added
little that was conclusive to the theory of revolution or counter-
subversion. Fought out on a vast scale with modern armaments
on both sides, it was at least vicariously an international rather
than an internal war. If it had any effect, it was to strengthen
somewhat the impression that the weak could successfully use
their own strength to resist the strong. Much more important
was its role as a cause to which for 'revolutionaries' within the
United States might rally. Without it, they could not so easily
have made the adjustment of directing their undefined hostility
against their own government. The already violent state of large

American cities, too, fostered the acceptance of the concept of 'urban guerrillas'—a concept particularly attractive to the radical wing of the Black movement, as it joined their urge for violence to a theoretical justification for tactics based on their own areas of strength.

To a large sector of the youth movement, however, 'revolution' as a shorthand for their own liberation and gratification in face of the resistance of their elders was interpreted in a characteristically individual manner. It was the first time that the element of humour had entered the concept, and it was this element that authority found hardest to understand or to forgive. In the new sense, revolution was not only deadly serious, it was also fun. Anarchical only in the sense that it revived the tradition of resistance to civil authority basic to the creation of the United States and restated for the nineteenth century by Thoreau,[39] the new movement did not seek to sacrifice the gains of industry and technology. Cameras, tape recorders, record players accompanied youth in their various lives, and even in their street fighting.[40] In taking as their slogan the adjuration of Emerson to 'do your own thing'[41] they did wish to ensure that the products of a consumer society were used to better the human being as a human being. The statement of these goals was well set out in writings of the 'underground', such as those collected in 1968 by 'Free' in *Revolution for the Hell of It*.[42] Their concept of revolution was:

> Revolution is in your head. You are the Revolution. Do your thing.

But there was a warning too.

> The possibility of violence will be greatly reduced. There is no guarantee that it will be entirely eliminated. *This is the United States, 1968, remember. If you are afraid of violence you shouldn't have crossed the border.*

To summarize, therefore, there are four main strands current in the present-day concept of revolution. All have much in common. One is basically economic. Revolution, according to it, is primarily a social phenomenon, resulting in the main from economic causes. On what these causes are, there is no agreement. The largest group holds with Marx that revolution results from increasing misery. A small group holds with de Tocqueville that it results from increasing prosperity, and with the recent developments in the youth movement discussed above it may well be that this view will return to favour. Meanwhile the dominant non-Marxist sociological trend is towards a combination of the two: the so-called 'J-curve' advanced by Davies,[43] or a period of increasing prosperity terminating in a situation which gives rise to demands which the government can no longer fulfil. It is this concept that lies at the basis of the economists' term, the 'revolution of rising expectations', which has minimal political connotations.

A second view is that revolution is a primarily social phenomenon, but one which arises from the failure of society to meet the demands put upon it. Present in the work of Edwards and Pettee, this concept received its most recent theoretical formulation in 1964 in Chalmers Johnson's *Revolution and the Social System*.[44] Significantly, Johnson has broken away from the sociological obsession with the 'great revolutions' to present a six-fold typology of revolutionary movements. These are: jacquerie; millenarian rebellion; anarchistic rebellion; Jacobin-Communist revolution; conspiratorial *coup d'état*; and militarized mass insurrection. Though this typology suffers from a certain lack of theoretical rigidity, in that its categories are not clearly related to the matrix of social causes advanced and there are gaps in that matrix that might be filled, Johnson's use of it suggests that there is much value in his general concept of revolution. This is of a state of social change brought about by multiple dysfunction in society, the act of revolt itself being precipitated by identifiable 'accelerators'. In an article published in 1966, the historian Lawrence Stone spoke warmly of the value this work could have for the historian.[45]

The third view is that revolution is a phenomenon based on the individual's sense of alienation from society. This was the view advanced by Talcott Parsons and it was also supported by Robert Merton.[46] In different ways, it has the merit of being compatible with the work of both the behavioural psychologists and of the psychoanalysts. So wide is the range even of 'normal' human behaviour, however, that political scientists have on the whole fought shy of its implications. The exceptions will be discussed later.

The last view, in the tradition of Aristotle, Machiavelli and Locke, is that revolution is a political phenomenon, concerned with the displacement of political power.[47] To it relate all the other aspects, for without the element of political change, economic, social and psychological changes would not be distinguishable in any real sense as 'revolutionary'.

As ever, assessment of each of these views is impeded by the doctrinal element. Revolution is nothing if not emotional. Basic to it are questions of the legitimacy of regimes and the propriety of force in human relations. Today, revolution seems generally 'acceptable' in that successful revolutionaries are normally accorded acceptance as having a degree of prior legitimacy for their actions. In many cases—even the Cuban one—this occurs only after success had been achieved, but the prospect of having to reclassify movements mentally at a later date clearly alarms many who like to have all their ideas neatly arranged for all time. The choice for them seems to lie between uncritical acceptance that revolution is socially beneficial at times, or rigid classification of actual movements by the criterion of whether or not they are favourable to their own interests. In consequence, in apposition to the four concepts listed above, there still survives one that is more ancient than any: the belief that revolution (at least against one's own interests) is an impious defiance of the will of the state or of the people, and hence contrary to the proper order of things. It is safe to say that this view, at least, will survive as long as human beings continue to resort to violence against one another. For as we have seen, it is not only basic to human society, but also to the survival of revolutionaries themselves.

7/The Possibility of Prediction

Prediction and self-fulfilment

It is scarcely surprising—given their importance to the welfare and even the survival of individuals—that from the earliest times men have devoted much effort to attempts to predict revolutions. The fact that they were so sudden, spasmodic and drastic, only made men more eager to do so.

About the earliest systems of prediction we know a lot, though little or no work has been done in testing their basic assumptions. The assassination of Julius Caesar, the murders of Caligula and of Claudius, are said by Roman historians to have been preceded by signs and auguries, involving such disparate phenomena as the flight of eagles, lightning bolts and the birth of two-headed calves. How much was known about these events before the fact of assassination we do not know, though Claudius for one clearly acted in such a way as suggests that he knew his days were numbered.[1] The warning addressed by the soothsayer to Julius Caesar in Shakespeare's play, is also based on historical evidence.[2] It must be taken seriously, for there are modern counterparts. Of one kind, there was the prophecy of Jeane Dixon, documented as far back as 1962, concerning the assassination of President Kennedy.[3] Of another, there was the warning given to General Suharto of Indonesia that he must go to the mouth of the river and pray on the night of September 30, 1965. His absence saved him from the massacre of the leading Indonesian generals by the abortive Communist revolt that night, and in due course he emerged as the new ruler of his country.[4]

In the latter case, involving a large-scale conspiracy, there clearly are possible circumstances in which news, more or less specific, could have leaked out in advance. The defects of conspiracies, noted by Machiavelli, render them very vulnerable to penetration by efficient intelligence agents, public or private. This, the method of prediction employed by governments, certainly dates back to the beginning of human history. Its weaknesses are its dependence on assessment of individual behaviour by unspecialized intuition, often by men whose main virtue is loyalty rather than sensitivity; its own liability to penetration, and, at worst, overload with an excess of information about possibilities, only one or two at a time of which can be selected for counterattack.

The former case, however, clearly does not fall within this category. Fortunately it is not within the province of the social scientist in his professional capacity to pass judgement. Yet in view of the origins of the word 'revolution' in fifteenth-century Italy, and its association with prophecy, more than a passing interest attaches to it. The behaviour of rulers is crucial. Extra-national criteria are essentially unpredictable, and unpredictability is a powerful asset for a ruler threatened by conspiracy. Certainly, behaviour which historians retrospectively attribute to political sagacity, has often been, and was at one time generally, based on techniques of divination. After all, Johannes Kepler, the father of modern astronomy, was the inventor of no less than eight new astrological aspects. And as his contemporaries sought signs of reassurance in troubled times, so do a great many more today.[5]

Giving weight to external influences, whether they be of the planets or of impersonal economic forces, implies that the existence of the human being in the universe is an ordered one. Over the centuries the limits of the social universe have varied, sometimes expanding, sometimes contracting. The rationalization of the concept of revolution which we have noted as occurring during the eighteenth century has never been complete. Significantly, prediction was not eliminated from it along with the concept of the universe on which it had been based. Though the *philosophes* did not foretell the French Revolution because of a forthcoming conjunction of planets, they did foretell it on the basis of their observations of society. France, they asserted, was overdue for a revolution, and by revolution they meant something like the English Civil War.[6] By developing a climate of opinion in which this was accepted, they favoured the course of events which actually ensued, and their prophecies therefore contained an element of self-fulfilment.

It is important to remember this, for if there is any field of research in which the element of self-fulfilment should be guarded against, it is this one. Justification may be much less important to revolutionary leaders than the prospect of success. A secular concept of revolution seems every bit as satisfactory when used as justification as does the idea of divine order or the unity of the universe.

The nineteenth century was the heyday of those who predicted revolutions on the very slightest of evidence. Most of them forgot that revolution, by its very nature, is a two-sided contest; that the prophecies that they made would be read, not only by those whom they sought to incite, but also by those who would wish to stop them. Quite naturally, nineteenth-century rulers, like fifteenth-century princes, listened to the voices of their soothsayers. If they were intelligent and skilful, they acted to forestall the conjunctions of interests which might give rise to dissension. This did increase the degree of unpredictability somewhat, at a time when the emergence of the disciplines of sociology and psychology were unwilling to accept the possibility of irrational phenomena, and so tended to ignore them. Lacking a rational alternative, it is not surprising that reform-minded thinkers were attracted to the implacable predictive doctrine of Marxism.

Marxism was predictive in that it maintained that revolution would occur at a particular moment in historical development. It had the added advantage, for the purpose of subsequent 'justification', of being vague on the circumstances (other than economic recession) and attaching no time limit to its predictions. This was just as well. No revolutions were associated with the recession of 1890, and the relation of others to that of 1907 was never sustained. Proletarian revolution did not break out in England, and eventually its theoretically predicted primacy in this respect was upstaged by the events of 1917. Finally, as an interesting commentary on the way history has of making fools of social scientists, the world's second 'proletarian' revolution occurred, of all places, in desert and nomadic Outer Mongolia. It is only fair to note that this revolution, which was engineered and assisted by the Soviet Union, was the first of a number in the twentieth century which have recently been given the useful designation of 'inspired' revolutions by Kornhauser.[7]

Outside the Marxist camp, of course, the meaning of prediction was itself obscured by the growing dissension as to what the term 'revolution' actually meant. It is certainly no easier in this respect for us today. Scholars who have sought to understand the phenomenon better have characteristically concentrated on the causes, the social forces generating support for revolutionary movements. This is the most difficult angle of approach. The magnitude of the research implied and the number of variables to be precisely identified are immense. The smallest error can have the most important consequences in assessing a movement whose active phases are normally compressed into a period of no more than a few weeks.

Sociologists educated in the tradition of Max Weber, Emile Durkheim and Talcott Parsons are certainly not unaware of the role of the individual in the crises of human society.[8] But their primary preoccupation has been to establish a general theory of the mechanics of society. They have had, perforce, to establish guidelines for study across the entire field of human behaviour. Their time has been spread correspondingly thin.

Types of group behaviour

Of the three types of group behaviour important to the

assessment of revolution—the actions of the leaders, of the crowd and of the ruling élite—the sociologists have concentrated almost exclusively on the last. Yet each is important, and none of the three groups can be considered wholly in isolation.

Since social psychology has grown out of the study of the individual, and the transfer of concepts from the study of the individual to the study of groups imposes substantial limitations on, and modifications of, techniques, the ability to get reliable information on the motivation of each of the three groups has necessarily proceeded unequally. In point of time, the study of the revolutionary leader probably came first. Not only is biography one of the most significant modern forms of self-expression, but it has deep roots in the past, as does autobiography, as Caesar's *De Bello Civico* bears witness.[9] Still, clinical study (other than that employed by untrained agents of government) is subject to the serious limitation that it operates entirely after the event, and must continue to do so, owing to the ambiguous legal standing of the prospective revolutionary in any society, whether his own or another.

The study of the crowd, then, was the first to be advanced in modern times. Reference has already been made to the seminal work of Gustave Le Bon.[10] Le Bon's basic thesis was that crowd behaviour was essentially recapitulatory: that in the crowd milieu the individual reverted to a pattern of behaviour characteristic of primitive man. As a member of a 'herd' he was absolved from individual responsibility and free to follow his primitive instinct to fight and to kill. It was to many an attractive theory, both because of its simplicity and because of its ethical overtones. It probably expresses with fair accuracy the general popular opinion of crowd behaviour today.

In 1921, however, Le Bon's thesis came under attack from Sigmund Freud in *Group Psychology and the Analysis of the Ego*.[11] Le Bon, he said, while deserving full credit for many important insights, had failed to consider the important aspect of the crowd's relationship to its leader. The individual identified with the leader by fixing his libido upon him as a father-substitute. Not only did he thereby absolve himself from responsibility, he was also thus motivated to place his loyalty to the group before that of wider social groups. Other aspects of Freudian theory gave rise, further, to the idea of a 'collective neurosis', which was freely used to explain crowd behaviour in an age when totalitarian regimes were eager to harness and exploit the energy it provided. (A derivation from this is the 1963 work of Hannah Arendt, *On Revolution.*[12])

But in advancing his theory of identification, Freud had inconveniently raised the key question of what was the driving force of the leader himself. Freud—at least as far as revolutionary leaders were concerned—treated the issue as a hot potato. It was the totalitarian leader that became the subject of clinical attention. Though in view of his often revolutionary origins there was reason to suspect that totalitarian inclinations might be a standard revolutionary attribute, there was yet sufficient difference between the careers of, for example, Stalin, Hitler and Mussolini, and those of Lenin, Robespierre and Garibaldi, to suggest that this assumption might have been questioned.

In the 1950s a generation of clinical work on individual subjects gave rise to the important collective study of *The Authoritarian Personality.*[13] Identification of a concept so usefully applicable to any consideration of leadership had an inevitable effect on basic assumptions about the behaviour of historical figures. It influenced, though not directly, the prevailing concern with the role of the military in politics, deriving from the historical work of Alfred Vagts.[14] Recently, in a study entitled *The Revolutionary Personality* (1967), E. V. Wolfenstein became the first to apply the concept of authoritarianism in the revolutionary field. Dealing with three individuals as different as Lenin, Trotsky and Gandhi, he raised a number of questions of much interest, which are bound to form the subject of future detailed research on others.[15]

It remains an open question, however, as to whether revolu-

tionaries really do have distinguishing psychological characteristics. Their distinctive attribute, after all, is their political
rather than their social specialization. It seems quite probable
that the revolutionary, leader as well as follower, is 'normal'
within the very broad degrees of freedom that that term implies.

Meanwhile the sociologists have not been idle. Much work
has been done on the sociological theory of mass movements, of
which one of the most recent is that of Neil Smelser, *Theory of
Collective Behavior* (1962).[16] Like other works in the field, this
derives from the concept of *anomie*, or alienation from society,
first propounded by Durkheim.[17] The application of this concept to the field of political science came to most political
scientists through the comparative work edited by Almond and
Coleman, *The Politics of the Developing Areas* (1960).[18] In their
hands, however, the concept of anomie underwent a profound
modification. What they termed 'anomic' groupings—riots,
demonstrations, strikes and the like—were defined in terms that
seriously limited the element of alienation while introducing
other criteria of definition. As 'sudden spontaneous irruptions
from the society into the polity' they could certainly be identified with specific phenomena which the student of revolution
would wish to delimit and assess. To do so, however, he would
not only have to examine the circumstances of alienation, but
also those making for suddenness and spontaneity. Helpfully,
Smelser suggests that the basic link lies in the transference of the
object of action when a specific course is found to be blocked,
such transference following a definable course through a matrix
of possibilities. Here, too, further important work is to be
expected in the near future.

'Great revolutions' and change

In the case of the concept of revolution, however, the
application of such ideas has been handicapped by a natural
division of opinion on what that concept currently is. The ruling
consensus (though, as we shall see, one that is now once again

being modified), is that revolution is properly definable only in terms of the so-called 'great revolutions'. Other forms of political violence, it has recently been suggested, should be subsumed under the definition of 'internal war'.

Both are clearly historical phenomena well worthy of the attention of the political scientist. But in the case of the 'great revolutions' their complexity, their ideological significance and the need to relate them to long chains of both causes and effects, make them particularly unsuitable as the starting point of any investigation. So too does the fact that there are very few of them. Nevertheless, their importance has meant that much has been written on them, and the preoccupation of sociologists with 'grand theory' has focused their attention on big problems.

In 1928 Lyford P. Edwards, in *The Natural History of Revolution*,[19] set the scene for the non-Marxists with the early statement that revolution was a phenomenon of social rather than political significance. '. . . the overthrow of the monarchy and feudal system in France was not caused by the French Revolution. The Revolution simply made evident the fact that the real power in France had passed into the hands of the middle class.' Whether his echo of Marx was conscious or unconscious, the fact was that he rejected all other movements and events as being unworthy of the name. 'Of course the so-called revolutions that so persistently afflict the Balkan states and the Latin American republics are not revolutions in this meaning of the word, but mere outbreaks of lawlessness leaving the institutions of the countries concerned virtually unchanged', he wrote. 'They mean no more than elections in more stable societies. And elections are themselves mere substitutes for civil war. It seems, on the whole, more profitable, even if less interesting, to count noses rather than break heads.'[20]

But of course the essence of revolution is that men do stop counting noses and do break heads. Edwards did not lose sight of this fact in discussing the 'great revolutions' but his treatment of it was cursory compared with that of other social phenomena.

The process of revolution, for him, began with 'the transfer of the allegiance of the intellectuals'. Their services were withdrawn from the *ancien régime* while their vision was turned to the type of new society that could be established. The revolution itself was 'a reintegration of society'. 'There is not less government during a revolution, there is more government.'[21] The fall of the *ancien régime* (itself treated vaguely and almost incidentally), brought an increase in mental and physical mobility, a brief period of optimism, and a diminution in conventional crime. In this period the radicals came to the fore, and soon, being dedicated and unified, assumed control of the government. Having done so, these men were ready to act in the absolute confidence born of faith, and were, by definition, the strongest men in society. So they used their power ruthlessly, achieving striking success in the objectives they set themselves. There followed a period of 'Terror'—an organized plan for the creation of new government—in which the deaths of victims became incidental to the effect it had on the co-ordination of society. Finally, this period being so intense that human nature was unable to stand the strain, there came a return to normality, often under the same rulers as before.

It will be seen that Edwards's scenario for the 'great revolutions' follows the course of the French Revolution closely. By 1938, when it was adopted simultaneously by the historian Crane Brinton and the sociologist George Sawyer Pettee, some modifications had become obvious. Thus though Brinton, whose work had an immense impact and may even be said to have created the image of revolution for a whole generation of scholars, followed French Revolutionary terminology (e.g. 'Thermidor', for the period of return to normality), he was much more cautious in delineating differences between the French model and the English, American and Russian experience. Furthermore Brinton specifically warned other scholars not to take the model as being definitive,[22] a warning which they have often failed to heed.

Taking Brinton as a starting point, there have been various individual studies of 'great revolutions' other than the classic four. One of the most recent attempts to compare these is that of Leiden and Schmitt. In their book, *The Politics of Violence*, they deal specifically with Mexico, Turkey, Egypt and Cuba.[23] It is interesting to note that they have retreated, in the course of this, from the assertion of Edwards that revolution as a term should be reserved for these rare phenomena alone. In fact, the definition of revolution which they adopt is that of the present author, which deliberately includes the broadest possible ranges of successful, violent political change, within which practically all other concepts of revolution fall, including the South American and Balkan.[24]

The reasons for this are clear. They may be easily seen in the very justifications of limitation advanced by Pettee:

> I have not referred very much to the minor revolutions. From the great revolutions to such palace revolutions as Macbeth's murder of Duncan one could make an unbroken series of graded cases. But only the great ones give us any chance to estimate the importance of all the factors. The apparently latent factors in the social system may play an important but undeterminable part in any partial revolution. In various crises society may be disorganized with reference to any one of its axes of organization, as a depression or inflation may disorganize the economic system. But only in a great revolution is it disorganized on all its axes. Therefore only in a great revolution does it come entirely apart, with all its internal forces revealed in the same light. Therefore it would seem that an adequate understanding of the partial revolutions can be arrived at only under the guidance of a theory of the total revolutions, because only the latter can give us a full picture of the complexity of forces which make an organized society what it is.[25]

It is one thing to lay open the full complexity of the internal forces of society. It is another to be able to assess accurately the strength and direction of individual forces. Such an assessment is bound to be achieved most accurately through the study of much simpler historical events. Certainly the hypotheses on which study is based must also be applicable to the 'great revolutions' if they are to have universal validity. But no theory based on the 'great revolutions' alone is likely to avoid dependence on personal and intuitional judgements, and, as Pettee himself says, any theory that is to be of use must not make the explicable inexplicable.

This warning was not heeded, as we have seen. In consequence, sociological tradition developed a split view. Basic research and the development of grand theory concentrated on the aspect of mass movements and the organization of violence. In the middle of this there was embedded a small group of ideas on the 'great revolutions' which stressed their uniqueness and unpredictability. It was for the ordinary scholar as if he were an astronomer attempting to build a theory of stellar combustion on observations of a handful of super-novae. Besides the understanding of 'the complexity of forces which make an organized society what it is' was in any case partially available from the study of organized society. And such study showed that many of the social changes of the 'great revolutions' had their counterparts in societies unaffected by violent political change.

For the political scientist, the basic understanding of the dynamics of violent political change is only attainable through study of all its aspects and of all the occasions on which it occurs. When this is done, the 'great revolutions' will not be left out. To quote Pettee again:

> Of course no social revolution is ever likely to take place without a coup d'état at some point. When social changes do take place without any political crisis they are not revolutions. But a social revolution cannot be grasped

through a study of the change of government affected. Anyone who tries to study the French Revolution from a purely constitutional angle will find not one but many coups d'état. A social revolution includes coup d'état as part of its process, but coups d'état can, and do, occur independently. There are many possible objectives for the coup d'état besides the reconstitution of the state.[26]

In the present author's *A Study of Revolution* an attempt has been made to show how the political concept of revolution does in fact gain in depth and understanding by the broader study suggested above. Concentrating on the fact of political change (the 'revolutionary event') will not give an explanation of the complex of social changes with which Edwards and Pettee were concerned. But it will give a greater understanding of the political core to which they relate. This approach did not, however, derive from a rejection of the limited use of the term 'revolution', but from recognition that in general use the traditional concept was by no means dead. Not the least of the reasons why this should be so was the fact that professional revolutionaries in all parts of the world claim it to dignify and ennoble their own movements, as in the case of the Brazilian revolution of 1964. To some extent this is supported by the widespread popular metaphorical usage of the word 'revolutionary', thus further blurring the political implications of the term.

Significantly, while attention was focused on the 'great revolutions', neither they nor indeed revolutions generally became any more predictable. Few onlookers, either in the East or in the West, drew from the course of the 26th July Movement in Cuba the deduction that a major revolution was in progress. And reasonably so, for the people who led it did not know at the time that that was what they were making.[27] Not until they got into power were they able to follow the lead of Mussolini and Hitler in using the force of the state to reconstitute society. In adopting a programme of radical social change, then, they abandoned their original power-base and sought to constitute another. Russians well-grounded in theoretical Marxism predicted that this would be disastrous. Finally, widespread social change did not take place as result of the one revolution where many would have predicted it, in France in 1958.

'Internal war'

But before, in our apparent helplessness, we turn back to the astrologers (and we could do worse), we should take one last look to see where in the conspectus of revolutionary phenomena the research methods of the social sciences have been applied. There is, indeed, such a place, though the literature dealing with it is as yet so sparse and scattered that it is difficult to assess in which of several possible directions progress is likely to be made. This is in the field of intra-societal violence, or as it is now termed, 'internal war'.

Research, as opposed to speculation, in this field began with the work of Pitrim A. Sorokin. As a recent exile from Russia, Sorokin produced in 1925 a study entitled *The Sociology of Revolution*.[28] In it he drew heavily upon his own experiences, and though it is an interesting work in this respect, it would be of limited concern to the historian of the concept of revolution if it had not marked the beginning of a much more ambitious programme of theoretical development and empirical research. The results of this research, set in the context of his own major theory of social change, were embodied in the third volume of Sorokin's monumental *Social and Cultural Dynamics*, with the sub-title *Fluctuation of Social Relationships, War and Revolution*.[29]

Sorokin takes as his field of study 'most of *the recorded internal disturbances of importance*, from the relatively small disorders to the biggest revolutions' in Greece, Rome, France, Germany, England, Italy, Spain, the Netherlands, Byzantium, Poland, Lithuania and Russia. 'The very fact of its mention in the annals of history is considered a sign of the importance of the disturbance.'[30] He then proceeds to analyse these disturbances qualitatively and quantitatively.

> Of these quantitative aspects four seem to be particularly important: (1) the proportional extent of the *social* (not merely geographical) area of the disturbance (social space); (2) the proportion of the population involved actively in the disturbance (for and against it); (3) the duration of the disturbance; (4) the proportional intensity (the amount and sharpness of violence and the importance of effects) of the disturbance.[31]

These variables were assessed on scales of varying widths, which could be adjusted so that the relative importance of each seemed to be in harmony. As Sorokin said, 'Other conditions being equal, the greater the proportional extent of the social area of the disturbance, the greater the proportion of the population involved in it, the greater its intensity and the longer its duration, then the greater is the comparative magnitude of the disturbance.'[32]

Since Sorokin wrote, the appearance of the work of Lewis F. Richardson on *Statistics of Deadly Quarrels*[33] has enabled the social scientist to improve on Sorokin's method in two ways: by establishing a precise measure of the magnitude of quarrels in terms of the number of casualties incurred, and by developing the use of logarithmic scales to aid immeasurably the relation of small to large numerical variables. But this is not to criticize the soundness of Sorokin's method, which, as when applied by Quincy Wright to the study of international war, yielded a vast amount of information of great importance.[34]

Qualitatively Sorokin set a precedent, which Chalmers Johnson[35] was to follow, in distinguishing between five different types of disturbances (in Johnson's case, six). The main types were: the predominantly political; the predominantly economic; nationalist and separatist; religious; or those with 'limited objectives'. A residual category was reserved for those in which the objectives were mixed. As in Johnson's case, the importance of this all-embracing system of classification is that it leaves open the question of the meaning of the word 'revolution', which is in Sorokin's writing generally avoided except as the title of the field of research.

The first conclusion Sorokin drew from his analysis was deceptively simple, but of great importance, namely: that there had been a surprisingly large number of them. It must be borne in mind that Sorokin was dealing only with happenings 'which violated the existing social order and laws of the period and of the society in which they occurred'.[36] Secondly, he observed that there was wide variation between the societies chosen, some exhibiting peaks of disturbance and quiescence and others a relatively smooth profile. He calculated, however, 'that on the average one notable social disturbance happens in about six years'.[37] No nation is exceptional. 'All nations are orderly and disorderly, according to the times.'[38] In intensity of violence, the only notable exception was Russia, where violence appeared to be more intense when it occurred. But on the other hand a pattern of lesser intensity was observable in the cases of Byzantium, England and Italy. Only five per cent of all the 1622 events occurred without any overt violence. So 'he who aspires for (*sic*) a disturbance must be ready to see violence and to be a witness or victim or perpetrator of it. This is true for all nations and groups.'[39] On the other hand, the average duration of most events was very short. 'Thus *most of the internal crises in the life process of a social body . . . come and pass their acute stage within a period of a few weeks.*'[40]

These are but some of Sorokin's observations. In placing them within the larger context of social change, he was, interestingly enough, concerned with giving rigorous examination to a cyclical concept of revolution. Since he was a sociologist and not a political scientist, the cycles he was concerned with were not those of Aristotle, but those proposed by Ferrari in his *Teoria dei periodi politici* (1874).[41] Ferrari had linked the incidence of revolution to a theoretical human generation of thirty-one years. Sorokin found the evidence for this to be thin. There was not even a relation to the incidence of war, in his view. 'There may be a very slight tendency for disturbances to occur more frequently in a period of war and in the years nearest war years, but the tendency is neither strong, consistent, nor quite tangible.'[42]

Sorokin, therefore, replaced the idea of revolution as a cyclical pattern on the one hand, and as a type of linear progress on the other, with a concept of his own which was entirely of the twentieth century. Revolution, for him, was a fluctuating tendency in society. He hypothesized that when all the variables were known, revolution would be found to be related to definite changes in social attitudes as between two 'ideal types' of society which he termed the 'Ideational' and the 'Sensate'.

Though it is not possible as yet to elucidate this relationship further, it is possible to make an observation which may make clear the importance of the question. Sorokin was dealing with disturbances of all types. If there is one thing that distinguishes revolution in the political sense from disturbances in general it is the fact of success. Already in the past few years a hint of this distinction has been appearing in the various works dealing with the general concept of 'internal war', though perhaps the avoidance of the term 'revolution' has most immediately tended to preserve the ambiguity of the theoretical formulations discussed earlier in this chapter. The definitive introduction to 'internal war' tends to deal primarily with military and social aspects, and so has the work of other scholars in the field.[43] These aspects now have to be related to the facts of political change and the social forces that accompany it.

It is possible, unfortunately, that the political agitation raised against the so-called 'Camelot' project, and similar projects, will discourage further progress in this.[44] Such agitation, as the foregoing will show, is based on a wholly erroneous idea of the possibilities of computation of events of immense complexity. Less forgivably, much of it is also based on two logical fallacies. The first of these fallacies is that greater understanding of the processes of political change will enable individual governments to predict and so forestall movements directed against themselves. The second is, that if this happens, it can stand in the way of the linear advance specifically designated as 'inevitable' by the advocates of certain forms of social change.

So we return at last to the original modern concept of revolution: a concept of sudden reversal and upheaval, within not a universal, but a social system of constraints and forces. In this concept lies the best chance for the development of a truly viable theory of revolution in political science. The concept of revolution as a social process can, and will, be related to it. The espousal of revolution as social programme or myth, however, has too long been entrusted to people who lack either the understanding or the humanity to relate their ambitions to the needs of human life. Revolution, in any recognizable form, is, and will remain, both dangerous and unpredictable. As long as it leads to violence, it is clearly a tendency that society should have outgrown. If a better understanding of political change leads to the elimination of violence, while at the same time ensuring a greater responsiveness of rulers to the needs of the ruled, then all the contributions of nearly five millenia of political development will not have been in vain.

8/Revolution in the World of the Future

The definition of terms

The story of the course of the development of the concept of revolution given here has necessarily been brief. It is, after all, a study of a concept, not of individual persons and movements. Hence there are many aspects of those movements which have not been dealt with here, and they will not be. It is, however, important, before leaving the subject, to define our terms as exactly as we may, and to attempt to ascertain their strengths and limitations. In doing so, we shall have to take account of a number of related issues which are not strictly germane to the nature of revolution itself.

First, though, it will be convenient to set out here those meanings which at one time or another have been attached to the word 'revolution' and which relate strictly to its own significance. In approximate historical order, they are the following.

1 *Defiance of authority.* Today we express this aspect by the terms 'rebellion', 'revolt' etc. But since the intention preceded the execution, it is the simple act of defiance which is the earliest historically identified. Fear of potential revolution even today often leads governments to use the term to designate movements which have not yet come to fruition, and may well never do so.

2 *Overthrow of rulers.* It is this that is the root meaning of the word revolution, since it is the political fact of the fall of a government and its replacement by another that distinguishes revolution from all other categories of event. The overthrow, however, must be one accomplished by the actual use or convincing threat

of violence, though such a pattern of violence may to some extent be ritualized. Aristotle distinguished a category of revolutions achieved through fraud rather than force, but such frauds generally involved the misuse of the state power itself. The apparent suddenness of events falling within this definition reflects the fact that this attribute dictated the choice of the modern word.

3 *Social dissolution.* Such a condition (called *stasis* by the Greeks) often results from the fall of rulers or of regimes. It may, however, occur independently, the formal institutions of government being apparently maintained but in fact powerless to check it. In such circumstances, there occurs a change in social and political relationships which affects deeply the political power and influence of the individual citizen. On the other hand, many writers have seen such a dissolution of the existing order, because of its completeness, as being a necessary prerequisite to the formation of a new kind of order which they desired. Regular use of the word in this sense was not established before the early eighteenth century.

4 *Revulsion against misused authority.* The overthrow of a tyrant was regarded as being of positive ethical value from very early times, though Aristotle attempted to study actual revolutions without making ethical judgements about their objectives. It was the only form of revolution recognized as valid in medieval Europe; all other unsanctioned uses of violence being regarded as defiance of authority, both human and Divine. As such, it had to some extent been superseded by the concept of simple change of rulers, before the justification of resistance to tyranny was first used in 1688 in connection with an event known to its supporters as a 'Revolution'.

5   *Constitutional change.* In Greece, with a wide variety of constitutional forms to choose from, overthrow of rulers was often seen as being a prerequisite to constitutional change. Such a change, of course, led to the reordering of a society and not its dissolution. Plato postulated that such changes of the constitutional order would follow a regular pattern, which Aristotle interpreted as a cycle. Similar possibilities for constitutional change existed at the time of the coinage of the word 'revolution', in the Italian city-states, but the concept of cycles was not durable and was in time assimilated to the eighteenth-century concept of linear progress. The first major instance of such constitutional change in modern times occurred in the formation of the Dutch Republic, but it became part of the broader meaning of the concept only about the time of the American Revolution.

6   *Reordering of society.* The fortunate absence of violence which accompanied the English Revolution of 1688 enabled observers to take at face value the claims of its proponents that their aims were wholly constructive. In the French Revolution, the relatively high level of violence that accompanied relatively widespread attempts at social engineering came as a shock. But few nineteenth-century revolutionaries doubted that enough had been achieved to make it worthwhile. Subsequently there have been two possibilities: either to 'play down' the role of violence or else to exalt it. Today the concept of revolution as social engineering or social reform is established as the second basic meaning of the word; by redefinition it has tended to become the more important one, though it lies at two removes from the first.

7   *Inevitable stage of development.* It is difficult to say when the concept of inevitability was first attached to the

social definition of revolution. Certainly it was already in existence by the French Revolution and is well illustrated by Condorcet. Economic determinism, however, formed a much more satisfactory basis for it, and its place in Marxist thought has been secure since 1848. Though there have been considerable differences as to the role of violence and the objectives to be sought, they have been defined in terms of the assumed inevitability of revolution in some form. In consequence, there has been a strong tendency for non-Marxist sociologists and economists to accept it as a basic postulate, and apply it to their own, more traditional, definitions of revolution. In this view, developed 'Western' states are seen as having already undergone their own historical revolutionary experiences: others have some similar experience yet to come.

8 *Permanent attribute of ideal order.* Product in the first instance of the natural desire of revolutionaries to ensure their own survival, the concept of permanent revolution as an ideal way of life became necessary to Marxists when they achieved power. Or, to put it another way, they and certain other former revolutionaries have found it convenient to redefine revolution as being government, interpreted in their own particular way. The conceptual link lay through the organization and methods in each case by which their government was made secure and their concept of social reform brought to fruition. Only Mao Tse-tung and his followers have actually tried to recreate as an engine of social control the conditions of armed struggle themselves, something hitherto assiduously avoided by all governments whatever their origins.

9 *Psychological outlet.* Revolutionaries must always have

felt that their actions in some way or another satisfied their individual drives. The significance of this component in the definition of revolution itself is, however, very recent. It cannot be dated prior to the 1920s, when elements of pyschoanalysis as explanation of human motivation displaced older concepts of reversion to primitive behaviour. It took a further two generations of acceptance before in the mid-1960s there came evidence that for the first time some proponents of political and social revolution were consciously aware of it as a vehicle for personal liberation.

We have already seen how these root meanings tend not to occur singly. The concept of revolution has embraced many things, not counting the host of metaphorical uses which in our own time have probably acted to no small extent to create a favourable 'image' of revolutionary changes of all kinds. It is for this reason that, though revolution has been regarded at various times as being a phenomenon *primarily* political, social, economic or psychological, it has never been regarded as being only one of these, and consequently it has always been only too easy for writers on politics to make use of the attribute or attributes of revolution which lay nearest to hand.

This process of selection is most influenced by the writer's purpose. But it does not take place in a vacuum. The selection takes place from among a range of ideas available, and these necessarily include conceptual schemes and philosophical systems in which the nature of revolution is only marginal. People therefore associate revolution with an 'outer layer' of concepts, from which—at least for the sake of precision—we should attempt to free it. There are great difficulties in doing so, as the ambiguity of human attitudes towards man's own violent instincts finds expression in a continual conflict between words and deeds.

Particular problems arise along the boundary between 'revolution' and 'nationalism'. Here in the absence of social controls that lie outside the boundaries of the state it is particularly easy for the advocate of national identity to embrace the methods of violence. Many individual national identities take as their point of reference some shared 'revolutionary' experience; a combination of efforts to shake off some form of outside influence or control. But at some point either before or during this experience a conflict has had to be resolved between those who believe that the society should find identity by pursuing its own inner ideals, and those who believe its higher purpose can only be served by adopting a programme of modernization conceived as having universal applicability. Such a conflict was that between the 'Slavophiles' and 'Westernizers' in Russia; and similar conflicts today have resulted in compromises differing as widely as between, say, Tanzania on the one hand and Ghana on the other.

For, as the Russian case shows, compromise is the only answer to the dilemma, and the fact of a 'revolutionary' experience does not involve its elimination. The choice of compulsory modernization involves contact with the outside world, which, in extreme cases, places strains on the system of control which are too great for it to handle. It therefore becomes necessary for the government to take account of the search for reassurance and stability evidenced by the citizens it has uprooted. Equally, as in the case of Indonesia under Sukarno, the pursuit of traditionalism, if carried too far, isolates the community from the outside world on which it has hitherto learnt to some extent to rely. Of course, much depends on location and the possibilities available for the intervention of outside forces. *Negritude* as a philosophical doctrine serves an essential psychological need in African states, if anything helping to enhance their political and diplomatic status by giving evidence of their actual cultural and physical attainments. 'Black pride' in the United States, where the psychological need for reassurance is much greater, is dysfunctional in the achievement of material goals because the black population represents only a small proportion of the whole.

In fact, it can be said that the success of revolution in forming national identity has been achieved in the past precisely in the degree in which it was externalized. A movement for independence, though revolutionary in form, provided the solidarity achieved in established states by resistance to another power in a foreign war. Today this option is seldom available. But the fact that it is not, does not mean that internally-directed revolutionary methods can achieve the same ends. In the main, the most that a nationalist can hope to gain by revolution today is power. But that, of course, may well be sufficient to enable him to carry out his main ends.

Unfortunately there is another response possible. This is the response of pessimism, the urge to destroy the fabric of society because it falls short of the ideal. This is not anarchism, since anarchism envisages an ideal state of society to the attainment of which certain revolutionary methods are held necessary. Stemming from the very nature of their beliefs, anarchists have never agreed on what those methods are, and a very large number in all ages have held that they were not necessary at all— that in the end human beings would realize their imperfections and build on their knowledge peacefully in a spirit of unselfishness. The urge to destroy is very different.

In the form of nihilism philosophical pessimism found expression in nineteenth-century Russia, and, it has been argued, formed an important element in the actions, as well as in the acceptance, of Hitler.[1] Though nihilism involves the destruction of politics along with society, it is clearly hard to form a vehicle for its political expression whose individual members are not motivated by some sense of self-preservation. The individual may destroy the world by suicide; he finds it much harder to persuade others to do the same. To this the ability of prominent Nazis to survive the death of their Führer amply bears witness.

Nihilism is, therefore, a concept that has little relevance to the practice or theory of revolution.[2]

It can be argued that men of today have the ability to destroy the world which their predecessors lacked. This is true, and it is no less a danger for the fact that it has not yet happened. It is, however, highly unlikely that as yet nuclear weapons will fall into the hands of revolutionaries, and as long as they do not, a great many people have an interest in seeing that the governments that do control them are not overthrown by force. If they are so overthrown, the nature of their military resources suggests that from within it can only be by their own armed forces.

At first sight, this is not encouraging. Militarism has long been, and is today, the motivation of the majority of successful attempts to overthrow governments by force. These changes are seldom followed by social change. In many instances they act to prevent it, which is, of course, precisely why they occur. If the concept of revolution as social change is accepted, the military is not a revolutionary, but a counter-revolutionary force. Here, therefore, the conceptual difference between the social and the political definitions of revolution presents real analytical problems.

These problems can be considerably mitigated if we remember that attitudes to revolution do not form part of the essential definition of militarism. Militarism is the glorification of the armed forces, either by themselves or by others, the representation of military values as being the embodiment of society.[3] Forcible intervention by the military in politics is, to the militarist, only a logical method of preserving those values. It is used relatively sparingly, since involvement in politics corrupts the military for its essential work of preserving the state against outside attack.

Intervention by the military, then, is only an aspect of a philosophy of conservatism. Conservatism, though present to some extent in the justifications of all revolutions, is only a prime revolutionary force where its adherents believe they must use violence to pre-empt radical change, or where they wish to reverse change relatively recently undertaken.

On the other hand, revolution, though associated in an historical sense with the emergence of liberalism, was never considered to be part of liberal doctrine. Liberalism was concerned with a programme of social change, not with the means with which that social change became possible, which might in common with other aspects of social behaviour be expected to become more acceptable as man evidenced the perfectability of which he was deemed capable. The weakness of nineteenth-century liberalism lay in its failure to realize the fragility of social obligations. Nor did its modification in the direction of welfare strengthen it, since it involved accepting pressures for change without satisfactorily coping with the need to establish a secure basis for the production of basic resources.

The paradox is that Marxism, in adopting the concept of materialism, at the same time embodied the wholly idealistic concept of revolution as a means of attaining material welfare. Actual revolutions are intensely disruptive to the material basis of society, and the more far reaching the effects of social engineering, the greater the waste of scarce natural resources that accompanies it. At one time it was thought that this waste was in fact an investment for future generations. Today the fallacy of this belief is apparent. It is not just the question of the loss of production for a few months or years, but the loss of capital for reinvestment. In the modern world a country that seeks industrial advancement to a status already attained by others simply cannot afford the luxury of revolution.

Revolution and political science

With the definition of revolution as a purely mystical concept we reach the point at which its practical applicability to politics becomes very questionable. It is therefore time to stop and to consider what political scientists should do to make the various concepts of revolution more precise to themselves as well as to others.

They would, firstly, be well advised to retain the term 'revolution' itself as a political term covering all forms of violent change of government or regime originating internally. This is not out of any mere spirit of antiquarianism for the oldest meaning of the term, but a simple recognition of the fact that it is the meaning most widely used in the modern world and there is no other available synonym for it.

Secondly, they would be well advised to study it. The change of governments by constitutional means has received much attention, and in consequence we know today a great deal about the personal and social factors that motivate it. There is even a word for this branch of political science—psephology—which reflects its established place as a recognized activity. Significantly, there is no such word for the study of extra-constitutional change, which suggests that something has been overlooked. The word *stasiology* has been used, but contains a certain potential for confusion. To make it quite clear that political scientists study revolution but have no professional interest in promoting it we might consider adopting instead the term *anacyclography*.

The word *coup* (or *coup de main*) may continue to be used for sudden political strokes of short duration, particularly in a military context. On the whole, however, it would be as well to avoid the term *coup d'état*, though it has been used frequently here. Technically a *coup d'état* is an action of government,[4] not of opposition, and its widespread use to refer to *coups* of all kinds leaves us without a term for what I have elsewhere called an 'official revolution'.

Then, since from the point of view of political science the social aspects of what is currently called 'social revolution' are subsequent to, and dependent on the political fact of change, this term should be carefully scrutinized. If it is to be used, it must be carefully defined in each context. Its value in sociology is undoubted. But for the political scientist it has the disadvantage of relating to a wide variety of forms of social change, only some of which are revolutions in the political sense.

When, therefore, the political scientist approaches social conditions which seem to him to indicate pressures for widespread change, it is incumbent on him to decide how he thinks those pressures are most likely to be resolved in political terms. For this he needs not only his customary level of acquaintance with the mode of operation of the political system of that country, but also far more exact concepts of unconstitutional political change than at present he possesses. He will then, hopefully, be better able to avoid preconceptions about the nature of desirable political change based on the experience of the society in which he lives, though it is important to say that such preconceptions are much less common among professional political scientists than among political writers generally.

For the experiences of societies in the future, though they may in some respects be similar, are in general likely to be very different. Technical inventiveness has given men and governments physical resources inconceivable a generation ago, but those resources come to men in developing societies in a fraction of a time that they did to their fellows in Europe. And, since man is a resourceful animal possessing the ability to learn from experience, the inhabitants of those countries can therefore be expected at the least to commit a rather different series of mistakes. They may well do better, if only because their social structures—though probably no less resistant to change than those of Europe—at least include far fewer devices from the early period of industrialization which is now obsolete.

The impact of this change is certainly enormously greater than any of the consequences of the French Revolution. Yet into it, political revolution as such may well not enter. Political scientists are likely, therefore, to prefer to eschew the term 'social revolution' altogether. It has been suggested here already that 'social change' or more specifically 'social engineering' are already at hand to describe the appropriate phenomena. These terms have the added advantage of enabling writers to distinguish from them those actions which have the limited political objective of enabling a new-fledged revolutionary government to stay in power. They will not effectively distinguish social changes which are the consequence of political revolutions from similar changes which are not. But in practice the present term does not do so either, in at least some cases because the confusion serves to conceal uncertainties of ideological interpretation.

Four other terms remain to identify major components of the concept of revolution.

'Revolt' clearly identifies attempts at political change which fail, or at least have not hitherto succeeded. The civil war in Nigeria, for example, is a revolt by this definition, but the Hungarian Revolution of 1956 was a revolution, for it did succeed, if only momentarily, in achieving control of the state.

'Constitutional change' refers to the political, as opposed to the social consequences of revolution. It embraces satisfactorily not only alterations of the formal instrument of government, but also shifts in the informal bargains, understandings and conventions that form the real constitution of all states. However it must be clearly stated in each case to which they refer.

'Violence' labels the essential ingredient that delimits revolutionary from constitutional action, and social change in a revolutionary context from social change in general.

'Millenarianism', though an awkward word, adequately covers those aspects of revolutionary change which are idealistically seen as leading to a reformation of society. Appropriately, it is a term equally applicable to sudden as to gradual transformation of political and social relationships.

With these terms, then, we can delimit with reasonable accuracy the nature of the phenomenon defined by the term 'revolution' in any existing usage. It would, however, at the same time be useful to revive the concept of 'social dissolution' under that label, though it is currently assumed that this is a concept which has no meaning in real terms. This assumption is based on the observation that human beings adapt their way of life with greater or lesser success to all conditions short of total annihilation. It is not intended to argue this question here. What it is intended to do is to point out that dissolution need not be total to be significant, and that social dissolution may be defined as that condition which governments seek by definition to avoid. It is perhaps not necessary to stress that one should try where possible not to accept at face value any claims of a government to be in some sense 'revolutionary' unless that term in that context means little more than 'progressive'. Even if a government habitually permits informal violence as a means of expressing, or of repressing interests, it cannot be said that this fact is one of its own attributes. If on the other hand it employs violence and institutionalizes it, then—again by definition—it transforms violence into force and brings it within the monopoly of force by the state.

Finally, it does seem advisable to avoid in scientific studies of political behaviour where possible all merely metaphorical uses of the terms 'revolution' and 'revolutionary', though they are so commonplace. One cannot, of course, avoid employing them in matter relating to terms employed in the other social sciences. Provided it is made clear that they do not mean the same thing in political terms, they can certainly be used in such a way as to eliminate all reasonable possibilities of confusion.

Ibid., p. 223.
Peter L. Shinnie, *Meroe, a Civilization of the Sudan*, Thames and Hudson, London 1967, pp. 165–9.
Herodotus, *Histories*, ed. Henry Cary, *Euterpe*, paras 162, 169.
Ibid., *Thalia*, paras 70–78.

2/Plato, Aristotle and the Romans

A. Andrewes, *The Greek Tyrants*, Hutchinson, London 1958, pp. 9–11.
Thucydides, *The Peloponnesian War*, trs. Rex Warner, Penguin Books, Harmondsworth, Middlesex 1956, p. 208.
Ibid., p. 209.
Plato, *The Republic*, trs. and ed. F. M. Cornford, Clarendon Press, Oxford 1955, cc. 29, 32.

5   *Aristotle's Politics*, trs. Benjamin Jowett, Clarendon Press, Oxford 1931.
6   Ibid., Book v, ii. 3–5.
7   Ibid., Book v, iv. 1–2.
8   Ibid., Book v, iv. 12.
9   Ibid., Book v, iv. 11.
10   Ibid., Book v, ix. 11–12.
11   Ibid., Book v, xii. 1–3.
12   A. W. Lintott, *Violence in Republican Rome*, Clarendon Press, Oxford 1968, p. 52.
13   See also Arthur Hatto, "Revolution: an Enquiry into the Usefulness of an Historical Term", *Mind*, New Series, 58, October 1949, p. 495.
14   Gordon Leff, *Medieval Thought; St Augustine to Ockham*, Penguin Books, Harmondsworth, Middlesex 1958, p. 175.
15   Polybius, *The Histories*, trs. and ed. W. R. Paton, Heinemann, London and Harvard University Press, Cambridge, Mass. 1922, 4 vols. See also F. W. Walbank, "Polybius on the Roman Constitution", *The Classical Quarterly*, xxxvii, No. 3, 4, July–October 1943, p. 73, and C. O. Brink and F. W. Walbank, "The Construction of the Sixth Book of Polybius", *The Classical Quarterly*, New Series, iv, No. 3, 4, July–October 1954, p. 97.
16   Polybius, Book vi, c. 9.7.
17   Cicero, *De Re Publica*, trs. C. W. Keyes, Heinemann, London and Harvard University Press, Cambridge, Mass., 1951. I. 42.
18   C. Suetonius Tranquillus, *The Twelve Caesars*, trs. Robert Graves, Penguin Books, Harmondsworth, Middlesex 1958, "Julius Caesar", c. 1.9.
19   P. Cornelius Tacitus, *The Annals of Imperial Rome*, trs. and intro. Michael Grant, Penguin Books, Harmondsworth, Middlesex 1956, p. 30; c.f. the thesis of Sir Roland Syme, *The Roman Revolution*, Clarendon Press, Oxford 1939.
20   E.g. Tacitus, *Annals*, under "Galba", "Otho", "Vitellius" and "Domitian".
21   The refutation of this charge was a major preoccupation of Augustine.

3/The Effects of Obedience

1   I Samuel 1. 14.
2   2 Kings 11.
3   Judges 3. 15–25.
4   I Peter 2. 17.
5   Matthew, 22. 21.
6   Augustine, *The City of Gods*, trs. John Healey, Dent, London 1934. See also Norman H. Baynes, *The Political Ideas of St Augustine's De Civitate Dei*, The Historical Association, London 1957.
7   For the development of political thought down to Aquinas see especially Walter Ullmann, *A History of Political Thought, The Middle Ages*, Penguin Books, Harmondsworth, Middlesex 1965.
8   P. Cornelius Tacitus, *On Britain and Germany*, trs. and intro. H. Mattingly, Penguin Books, Harmondsworth, Middlesex 1951.
9   *The Annals of the Kingdom of Ireland by the Four Masters; from the earliest period to the year 1616*, trs. J. O'Donovan, Hodges and Smith, Dublin 1851.
10 Alice Stopford Green, *History of the Irish State to 1100*, Macmillan, London 1925, p. 274.
11 Erwin I. J. Rosenthal, *Political Thought in Mediaeval Islam, an Introductory Outline*, Cambridge University Press, Cambridge 1962, p. 42.
12 Ibid., p. 106.
13 Ibid., p. 108; for more detail see Ibn Khaldun, *The Muquaddimah; an Introduction to History*, trs. F. Rosenthal, Pantheon Books, New York 1958.
14 Thomas Aquinas, *Selected Political Writings*, ed. and intro. A. P. d'Entrèves, Basil Blackwell, Oxford 1959, p. 31.
15 Ibid., Quaestio XL, Art. 1 (*De Bello*).
16 Ibid., Quaestio XLII, Art. 2 (*De Seditione*).
17 Ibid., p. 177.
18 John of Salisbury, *The Statesman's Book*, ... selections ... *from the Policraticus*, Russell and Russell, New York 1963.
19 Hatto, "Revolution: An Enquiry", op. cit.
20 Niccolò Machiavelli, *The Prince*, trs. George Ball, Penguin Books, Harmondsworth, Middlesex 1963, pp. 71, 103, 98.
21 Marsilius of Padua, *The Defender of Peace (The Defensor Pacis)*, trs. Alan Gewirth, Harper Torchbooks, New York 1956.
22 Machiavelli, *The Prince and the Discourses*, Random House, New York 1960, p. 398.
23 Ibid., p. 406 (Title to Bk III, c. iv).
24 Ibid., p. 410.
25 Ibid., p. 413.
26 Ibid., p. 414.
27 Ibid., pp. 416–32, 432; c.f. the compressed treatment of the same topic in *The Prince*, pp. 66–77 (Ch. xix).

28 Curzio Malaparte, *Coup d'Etat, the Technique of Revolution*, trs. Sylvia Saunders, Dutton, New York 1932; Feliks Gross, *The Seizure of Political Power in a Century of Revolutions*, Philosophical Library, New York 1958; Edward Luttwak, *Coup d'Etat, a Practical Handbook*, Allen Lane, The Penguin Press, London 1968; D. J. Goodspeed, *The Conspirators. A Study of the Coup d'Etat*, Macmillan, London 1962; David C. Rapoport, "Coup d'Etat, the View of the Men Firing Pistols", *Nomos VII: Revolution*, ed. Carl J. Friedrich, Atherton Press, New York 1966.

4/The Sense of Rebellion

1   Martin Luther, *Martin Luther: Selections from His Writings*, ed. and intro., John Dillenberger, Doubleday Anchor, Garden City, N.Y. 1961, p. 363 ff.

2   Jean Calvin, *Institutes of the Christian Religion*, ed. John T. McNeill, trs. Ford Lewis Battles, Westminster Press, Philadelphia 1960, II, p. 1485 ff.

3   Junius Brutus, (*pseud.*), *A Defence of Liberty against Tyrants, a translation of the Vindiciae contra tyrannos*, intro. by Harold J. Laski, Bell, London 1924, p. 66.

4   Ibid., p. 71.

5   Ibid., p. 76.

6   Ibid., p. 97.

7   Ibid., p. 98.

8   Ibid., p. 114.

9   C. V. Wedgwood, *William the Silent. William of Nassau, Prince of Orange, 1533–1584*, Jonathan Cape, London 1944, p. 224.

10 Ibid., p. 220.

11 James Harrington, *The Political Writings of James Harrington; Representative Selections*, ed. and intro. Charles Blitzer, Bobbs-Merrill, Indianapolis 1955, "A System of Politics delineated" etc., III. 7.

12 John Milton, "The Tenure of Kings and Magistrates", in *The Works of John Milton*, ed. Rev. John Mitford, W. Pickering, London and Little and Brown, Boston 1851, IV, p. 450. See also R. C. Latham, "English Revolutionary Thought", *History*, New Series, xxx, 1945, p. 38; Hatto, "Revolution: An Enquiry", op. cit.

13 John Locke, *The Second Treatise of Government . . . and a Letter concerning Toleration*, ed. and intro. J. W. Gough, Basil Blackwell, Oxford 1956, sec. 211–221.

14 It is well known that Jefferson dropped the most original one, that accusing the king of imposing Negro slavery on the colonies, out of deference to political considerations.

15 Text taken from Henry Steele Commager (ed.), *Documents of American History*, Appleton-Century-Crofts, New York 1958, p. 100.

16 Letter from Thomas Jefferson to Robert Weightman, June 24, 1826, cited in L. H. Butterfield, "July 4 in 1826", *American Heritage*, VI, 4, p. 14.

17 Edmund Burke, *Reflections on the Revolution in France* . . ., W. Watson and others, Dublin 1790.

18 Jean-Jacques Rousseau, *Political Writings*, Nelson, Edinburgh 1953.

19 Alexis de Tocqueville, *The Ancien Régime and the French Revolution*, intro. Hugh Brogan, trs. Stuart Gilbert, Collins/Fontana, London 1966, p. 35. See also the important article by Melvin Richter, "Tocqueville's contribution to the theory of revolution", in *Nomos VII: Revolution*, op. cit.

20 John Lukacs, *Decline and Rise of Europe: a study in recent history with particular emphasis on the development of a European consciousness*, Doubleday, Garden City 1965. Harold Lasswell, in *Politics; Who gets What, When, How*, The World Publishing Co., Cleveland and New York 1958, pp. 171–2, gives his reasons for considering it and the Russian as 'world revolutions' which were partly restricted and partly internalized.

21 de Tocqueville, op. cit., p. 40.

22 Joan Macdonald, *Rousseau and the French Revolution, 1762–1791*, University of London, The Athlone Press, London 1965.

23 Reference is to his actions rather than his works, but see Maximilien Marie Isidore de Robespierre, *Oeuvres complètes*, Leroux, Paris 1910–, 10 vols.

24 Denis W. Brogan, *The Price of Revolution*, Hamish Hamilton, London 1951, p. 8 ff.

25 Beginning with Lyford Paterson Edwards, *The Natural History of Revolution*, Russell and Russell, New York 1965, 2nd edn.

26 Peter Amann (ed.), *The Eighteenth-Century Revolution, French or Western?* D. C. Heath, Boston 1963, gives opposing points of view.

27 Crane Brinton, *The Anatomy of Revolution*, Vintage Books, New York 1952.

28 George Sawyer Pettee, *The Process of Revolution*, Harper, New York 1938.

5/The Theory of Inevitability

1 Thomas Paine, *Rights of Man. Being an Answer to Mr Burke's Attack on the French Revolution*, Dent, London and Dutton, New York 1930, p. 135.

2 Giuseppe Mazzini, *The Duties of Man and other essays by Joseph Mazzini*, Dent, London and Dutton, New York 1912, p. 251.

3 This, of course, is a modernism, c.f. Chalmers Johnson, *Revolution and the Social System*, The Hoover Institution, Stanford 1964, and the same author's *Revolutionary Change*, Little Brown, Boston 1966.

4 Burke, op. cit.

5 Domingo Faustino Sarmiento, *Life in the Argentine Republic in the Days of the Tyrants, or, Civilization and Barbarism*, Collier, New York 1961. (Sp. title *Facundo*.)

6 Ferdinand Lassalle, "Was nun?", in *Reden und Schriften*, Ludwig Maenner (ed.), R. Hobbing, Berlin 1926, p. 179 ff.

7   Karl Marx and Friedrich Engels, *Selected Works*, Foreign Languages Publishing House, Moscow 1962, I, pp. 21–65 ("Manifesto of the Communist Party").

8   C.f. Herbert Spencer, *Principles of Sociology*, abridged ed, Stanislav Andreski, Archon Books, Hamden, Conn. 1969.

9   Marx and Engels, op. cit., I, p. 120 (Introduction by Engels to "The Class Struggles in France 1848–1850".

10 Ibid., p. 243 ("The Eighteenth Brumaire of Louis Bonaparte").

11 Ibid., p. 135.

12 Ibid., II, p. 452.

13 Friedrich Engels, *Anti-Dühring's, Herr Eugen Dühring's revolution in science*, Foreign Languages Publishing House, Moscow 1962.

14 Priscilla Robertson, *Revolutions of 1848, a Social History*, Harper, New York 1960.

15 Marx and Engels, op. cit., I, p. 473 ("The Civil War in France").

16 James Joll, *The Anarchists*, Eyre and Spottiswoode, London 1964; see also Petr Alekseevich Kropotkin, *Memoirs of a Revolutionist*, James Allen Rogers (ed.), Doubleday, Garden City, New York 1962; the works of Mikhail Bakhunin now appearing in Archives Bakhounine/Bakunin Archiv, Internationaal Instituut voor Sociale Geschiednis, Amsterdam, T. Brill, Leiden 1969–; and Vernon Richards, *Errico Malatesta, his Life and Ideas*, Freedom Press, London 1965. For the mainstream of the anarchist tradition in the United States see Emma Goldman, *Anarchism and other essays*, Mother Earth Publishing Association, New York 1910. Of note as a formative influence is Pierre Joseph Proudhon, *Idée générale de la Révolution au xixe siècle*, Garnier, Paris 1851.

17 Ferrer's contribution to political anarchism was entirely as a victim; his intellectual contribution was to progressive education, see Francisco Ferrer Guardia, *The Origin and Ideas of the Modern School*, trs. Joseph McCabe, G. P. Putnam, New York 1913.

18 Gerald Brenan, *The Spanish Labyrinth, an Account of the Social and Political Background of the Spanish Civil War*, Cambridge University Press, Cambridge 1962.

19 General introduction to each of these may be found in the Thames and Hudson series "The Great Revolutions", especially J. Halcro Ferguson, *The Revolutions of Latin America*, 1963; Francisco Gabrieli, *The Arab Revival*, 1961, and Tibor Mende, *The Chinese Revolution*, 1961.

20 See Robert E. Quirk, *The Mexican Revolution, 1914–1915; The Convention of Aguascalientes*, Indiana University Press, Bloomington, 1960.

21 Goodspeed, op. cit., pp. 82–98.

6/The Attraction of Permanence

1   Vladimir Ilyich Lenin, *State and Revolution*, International Publishers, New York 1968. In the present work it is not possible to pursue all the ramifications of Lenin's contribution to the view of the Russian Revolu-

tion. Interested readers are advised to study the three volume edn. of *Selected Works*, Foreign Languages Publishing House, Moscow 1968.

2 Reference is to R. Palme Dutt, *Fascism and Social Revolution; A Study of the Economics and Politics of the Extreme States of Capitalism in Decay*, International Publishers, New York 1935, revised edn.

3 Trotsky's own account is of course now available in his *History of the Russian Revolution to Brest-Litovsk*, Gollancz, London 1966. But the main events were well enough known at the time. C.f. Louis Gottschalk, "Leon Trotsky and the Natural History of Revolution", *The American Journal of Sociology*, XLIV, No. 3, November 1938, p. 339.

4 James H. Meisel, *Pareto and Mosca*, Prentice-Hall, Engelwood Cliffs, N.J. 1965, pp. 15–17. A reminder of the continued significance of Machiavelli in Italian political thought can be found in the interesting study by Umberto Melotti, *Rivoluzione e Società*, Ed. Culturale, Milano 1965.

5 Georges Sorel, *Reflections on Violence*, trs. T. E. Hulme and J. Roth, intro. Edward A. Shils, The Free Press, Glencoe, Ill. 1950.

6 Gustave Le Bon, *Psychologie des Foules*, Félix Alcan, Paris 1895; Eng. trs. *The Crowd; a Study of the Popular Mind*, intro. Robert K. Merton, Viking Press, New York 1960. On the social composition of crowds in the French Revolution note George Rudé, *The Crowd in History; a Study of Popular Disturbances in France and England, 1730–1848*, John Wiley, New York 1964.

7 In 1944.

8 Curzio Malaparte, *Coup d'Etat*, op. cit.

9 From Laureano Vallenilla Lanz, *Cesarismo Democrático*, Caracas 1919.

10 Literature on the Mexican revolution is immense, but its ideologues were few, see however José Vasconcelos, *Que es la revolución?* Ed. Botas, Mexico 1937. Martin C. Needler, "Mexico, Revolution as a way of life", in his *Political Systems of Latin America*, Van Nostrand, New York 1964 will be found a helpful introduction. An interesting product of post-revolutionary reassessment, combining Marxist tradition and recent American sociology, is Eliseo Rangel Gaspar, *Hacia una Teoria de la Revolución Mexicana*, Talleres Gráficos de la Nación, Mexico 1964.

11 Peter Calvert, "The Institutionalization of the Mexican Revolution", *Journal of Inter-American Studies*, XI, No. 4, October 1969, p. 503.

12 Reference is particularly to the control of the army with the aid of the Gestapo, including the formation of the Waffen-SS.

13 Katharine C. Chorley, *Armies and the Art of Revolution*, Faber and Faber, London 1943, p. 11.

14 Ibid., p. 20.

15 See Max Caulfield, *The Easter Rebellion*, Four Square Books, London 1965.

16 As in the recent espousal of radical change by the episcopate in Peru.

17 Peter Calvert, *A Study of Revolution*, appendices.

18   Georg Wilhelm Friedrich Hegel, *Hegel's Philosophy of Right*, trs. T. M. Knox, Clarendon Press, Oxford 1962, p. 155, sec. 257–8. See also Herbert Marcuse, *Reason and Revolution; Hegel and the rise of Social Theory*, Routledge and Kegan Paul, London 1968, second edn.

19   Notably in the work of T. H. Green.

20   A view borrowed from the impression of economic incompetence strongly fostered at the time by John Maynard Keynes, *The Economic Consequences of the Peace*, Macmillan, London 1920, but compare the work of recent historians, especially Arthur M. Link.

21   A thesis strongly upheld by Goodspeed, pp. 65–6.

22   Stuart R. Schram (ed.), *The Political Thought of Mao Tse-tung*, Pall Mall, London and Praeger, New York 1963; see also Andrew C. Janos, "The Communist Theory of the State and Revolution", in Cyril E. Black and Thomas P. Thornton, *Communism and Revolution, The Strategic Uses of Political Violence*, Princeton University Press, Princeton 1964.

23   Condensed version available in Mao Tse-tung and (Ernesto) Che Guevara, *Guerrilla Warfare*, Cassell, London 1964.

24   Truong Chinh (*pseud*), *Primer for Revolt, the Communist takeover in Viet-Nam; A Facsimile Edition of The August Revolution and The Resistance Will Win*, intro. and notes Bernard B. Fall, Praeger, New York 1963; Vo Nguyen Giap, *People's War, People's Army*, Pall Mall, London and Praeger, New York 1965, second edn.

25   Bernard B. Fall (ed.), *Ho Chi Minh On Revolution: Selected Writings 1920–66*, Pall Mall, London 1967.

26   Abdul Haris Nasution, *Fundamentals of Guerrilla Warfare*, intro. Otto Heilbrunner, facsimile edn., Praeger, New York 1965.

27   Examples are Charles W. Thayer, *Guerrilla*, Michael Joseph, London 1963; John W. Pustay, *Counterinsurgency Warfare*, The Free Press, New York and Macmillan, London 1965; Peter Paret and John W. Shy, *Guerrillas in the 1960s*, Praeger, New York 1962, revised edn.

28   See José Martí, *The America of José Martí; Selected Writings*, trs. Juan de Onís, Funk and Wagnalls, New York 1968.

29   Thomas Edward Lawrence, *The Seven Pillars of Wisdom. A Triumph*, M. Pike with H. J. Hodgson, London 1926.

30   Frantz Fanon, *The Wretched of the Earth*, Penguin Books, Harmondsworth, Middlesex 1967.

31   Sigmund Neumann, *Permanent Revolution; Totalitarianism in the Age of International Civil War*, Pall Mall, London 1965, second edn. of *Permanent Revolution; the Total State in a World at War*, Harper, New York 1942.

32   C.f. Mehmet Beqiraj, *Peasantry in Revolution*, Cornell University Center for International Studies, Ithaca, New York 1966.

33   Notably, of course, France: see Patrick Searle and Maureen McConville, *French Revolution, 1968*, Penguin Books, Harmondsworth, Middlesex 1969. The French 'New Left' is in some respects more 'traditional'.

34 Kwame Nkrumah, *Neocolonialism, the Last Stage of Imperialism*, Nelson, London 1965, is derivative rather than creative. See also the same author's *Handbook of Revolutionary Warfare: a guide to the armed phase of the African Revolution*, Panaf Books, London 1968.

35 Ernesto (Che) Guevara, *Guerrilla Warfare*, Monthly Review Press, New York and London 1967.

36 Régis Debray, *Revolution in the Revolution*, Penguin Books, Harmonds-worth, Middlesex 1969.

37 Literature on this subject is naturally still sparse; a useful starting point is Régis Debray, "Latin America: the Long March", *New Left Review*, 33, September–October 1965, p. 17.

38 Daniel James (ed.), *The Complete Bolivian Diaries of Che Guevara and Other Captured Documents*, Stein and Day, New York 1968.

39 Henry David Thoreau, "Letter on Civil Disobedience" in *Walden and 'Civil Disobedience'*, New American Library, New York 1960.

40 United States National Commission on the Causes and Prevention of Violence, *Rights in Conflict, The Violent Confrontation of Demonstrators and Police in the Parks and Streets of Chicago during the Week of the Democratic National Convention*, Bantam Books, New York 1968. It seems now a far cry to this from the state of affairs described by Anthony Lewis and the *New York Times* staff as *Portrait of a Decade, the Second American Revolution* Bantam Books, New York 1965.

41 Ralph Waldo Emerson, "Self-Reliance" in *Essays: First and Second Series*, A. L. Burt, New York, Undated, p. 33.

42 Free (*pseud*. of Abbie Hoffman), *Revolution for the Hell of It*, The Dial Press, New York 1968, pp. 10, 107.

43 James C. Davies, "Towards a Theory of Revolution", *The American Sociological Review*, XXVII, No. 1, February 1962, p. 5; c.f. Richter, op. cit.

44 Chalmers Johnson, *Revolution and the Social System*, op. cit.

45 Lawrence Stone, "Theories of Revolution", *World Politics*, XVIII, No. 2, January 1966, p. 159.

46 See especially Talcott Parsons and Edward A. Shils (eds), *Towards a General Theory of Action*, Harper, New York 1962. Robert K. Merton, *Contemporary Social Problems; an introduction to the sociology of deviant behaviour and social disorganization*, Harcourt Brace and World, New York 1961.

47 C.f. Peter Calvert, "Revolution: the Politics of Violence", *Political Studies*, XV, No. 1, February 1967, p. 1.

7/The Possibility of Prediction

1 Suetonius, "Tiberius Claudius".

2 Ibid., "Julius Caesar".

3 Ruth Montgomery, *A Gift of Prophecy; the Phenomenal Jeane Dixon*, William Morrow, New York 1965, pp. 1–13.

4 Tarzie Vittachi, *The Fall of Sukarno*, Praeger, New York 1967, pp. 105–6.

5 Modern astrologers have attributed the Russian Revolution to the entry of Neptune into Leo, but associate revolutionary change generally with the planet Uranus, which was discovered in 1781. In March 1917 Uranus was on the Tzar's mid-heaven close to the place of his Sun, leading to a prediction that he should 'beware of sinister and seditious influences'. *Raphael's Prophetic Almanack for 1917*, W. Foulsham, London 1916. Not all Raphael's prophecies for 1917 were accurate however, and some were very wrong indeed.

6 Hatto, "Revolution: An Enquiry", op. cit.

7 William Kornhauser, "Revolution and National Development", paper delivered at Sixth World Congress of Sociology, Evian 1966.

8 Max Weber devoted much of *The Theory of Social and Economic Organization*, ed. and intro. Talcott Parsons, The Free Press, New York 1965, to identification and comparison of types of authority, but makes no special reference to the role of the revolutionary leader.

9 C. Julius Caesar, *The Civil War* etc., trs. Jane F. Mitchell, Penguin Books, Harmondsworth, Middlesex 1967.

10 Le Bon, *Crowd Behaviour*, op. cit.

11 Sigmund Freud, *Group Psychology and the Analysis of the Ego*, trs. James Strachey, Bantam Books, New York 1965.

12 Hannah Arendt, *On Revolution*, Faber and Faber, London 1963. See also Harold D. Lasswell, *Psychopathology and Politics*, Viking Press, New York 1960.

13 T. W. Adorno, Else Brunswik-Frenkel, Daniel J. Levinson and R. Nevitt Sanford, *The Authoritarian Personality*, John Wiley, New York 1964, 2 vols.

14 Alfred Vagts, *A History of Militarism; Civilian and Military*, Hollis and Carter, London 1959. See also Samuel E. Finer, *The Man on Horseback*, Pall Mall, London 1962.

15 E. Victor Wolfenstein, *The Revolutionary Personality; Lenin, Trotsky, Gandhi*, Princeton University Press, Princeton 1967. See also the influential Eric Hoffer, *The True Believer; thoughts on the nature of mass movements*, Harper, New York 1951, and the oddly named *World Revolutionary Elites; Studies in Coercive Ideological Movements*, ed. Harold D. Lasswell and Daniel Lerner, The M.I.T. Press, Cambridge, Mass. 1966.

16 Neil J. Smelser, *Theory of Collective Behavior*, Routledge and Kegan Paul, London 1962.

17 Emile Durkheim, *The Division of Labor in Society*, trs. George Simpson The Free Press, New York 1965. See also Sebastian de Grazia, *The Political Community, a study of anomie*, University of Chicago Press, Chicago 1963.

18 Gabriel Almond and James S. Coleman, *The Politics of the Developing Areas*, Princeton University Press, Princeton 1960.

19   Lyford B. Edwards, *The Natural History of Revolution*, op. cit., p. 7.
20   Ibid., p. 16.
21   Ibid., p. 107.
22   Crane Brinton, *The Anatomy of Revolution*, op. cit., p. 3.
23   Carl Leiden and Karl M. Schmitt, *The Politics of Violence: Revolution in the Modern World*, Prentice-Hall, Englewood Cliffs, N.J. 1968, p. 9.
24   Peter Calvert, "Revolution: the Politics of Violence", op. cit.
25   George Sawyer Pettee, *The Process of Revolution*, Harper Brothers, New York 1938, pp. xi–xii.
26   Ibid., pp. 27–8.
27   See, for example, the by no means hostile Robert Scheer and Maurice Zeitlin study, *Cuba, an American Tragedy*, Penguin Books, Harmondsworth, Middlesex 1964, rev. edn.
28   Pitrim A. Sorokin, *The Sociology of Revolution*, J. B. Lippincott Co., Philadelphia and London 1925.
29   Pitrim A. Sorokin, *Social and Cultural Dynamics, III: Fluctuation of Social Relationships, War and Revolution*, American Book Co., New York 1937.
30   Ibid., p. 385.
31   Ibid., p. 389.
32   Ibid., p. 340.
33   Lewis F. Richardson, *Statistics of Deadly Quarrels*, Stevens and Sons, London 1960. Indicators of domestic violence are to be found for various countries in Arthur S. Banks and Robert Textor, *A Cross-Polity Survey*, Harvard University Press, Cambridge, Mass. 1963 and Bruce M. Russett (ed.), *World Handbook of Political and Social Indicators*, Yale University Press, New Haven 1964.
34   Quincy Wright, *A Study of War*, University of Chicago Press, Chicago 1965, second edn.
35   Chalmers Johnson, *Revolution and the Social System*, op. cit.
36   Pitrim A. Sorokin, *Social and Cultural Dynamics III*, p. 403.
37   Ibid., p. 473.
38   Ibid., p. 475.
39   Ibid., p. 478.
40   Ibid., p. 479.
41   Giuseppe Ferrari, *Teoria dei periodi politici*, Milano-Napoli 1874.
42   Pitrim A. Sorokin, *Social and Cultural Dynamics III*, p. 489, c.f. Chorley, op. cit. See *inter alia* Ivo K. Feierabend and Rosalind K. Feierabend, "Aggressive Behaviors within Polities, 1948–1962; a cross-national study", *The Journal of Conflict Resolution*, x, No. 3, September 1966, p. 249; Frank H. Denton and Warren Philips, "Some Patterns in the History of Violence", *The Journal of Conflict Resolution*, xii, No. 2, June 1968, p. 182.
43   Harry Horace Eckstein (ed.), *Internal War, Problems and Approaches*, The Free Press, New York 1964; see also James N. Rosenau (ed.), *International Aspects of Civil Strife*, Princeton University Press, Princeton 1964

and the Princeton monographs of Andrew C. Janos, "The Seizure of Power, a Study of Force and Popular Consent", 1964, and Charles Tilly and James Rule, "Measuring Political Upheaval", 1965. For its theoretical interest in particular see also Raymond Tanter and Manus Midlarsky, "A Theory of Revolution", *The Journal of Conflict Resolution*, XI, No. 3, September 1967, p. 264.

44 Irving Louis Horowitz (comp.), *The Rise and Fall of Project Camelot*, The M.I.T. Press, Cambridge, Mass. 1967.

8/Revolution in the World of the Future

1 Hermann Rauschning, *The Conservative Revolution*, G. P. Putman's Sons, New York 1941, p. v.

2 Leiden and Schmitt, p. 74.

3 Vagts, p. 12.

4 OED: 'a sudden and decisive stroke of state policy; *spec.* a sudden and great change in the government carried out violently or illegally by the ruling power'.

Bibliography

Select Bibliography

1 Primary

AQUINAS, ST. THOMAS (1224–74), *Selected Political Writings*, ed. and intro. A. P. D'Entrèves, Basil Blackwell, Oxford 1959. Definitive statement for the mediaeval world of the right to overthrow a tyrant. Still significant in Catholic countries.

ARISTOTLE, *Politics*, trs. Benjamin Jowett, intro. H. W. C. Davis, Clarendon Press, Oxford 1931. First and still remarkably informative study of revolutions; develops thesis of their relationships to forms of government and postulates cycle of change.

BRINTON, CRANE, *The Anatomy of Revolution*, Vintage Books, New York 1952. Influential study of English, French, American and Russian revolutions, subsequently interpreted to support thesis that 'revolution' is applicable only to rare periods of social change.

'BRUTUS, JUNIUS,' (*pseud.*), *A Defence of Liberty against Tyrants*, a translation of the *Vindiciae contra Tyrannos*, intro. Harold J. Laski, G. Bell, London 1924. First work to indicate a specific revolution desirable, at the same time indicating who had authority to decide.

BURKE, EDMUND, *Reflections on the Revolution in France* . . . W. Watson and others, Dublin 1790. Most important statement of thesis that the disruption of society by revolution cuts short progress.

DE TOCQUEVILLE, ALEXIS, *The Ancien Régime and the French Revolution*, intro. Hugh Brogan, trs. Stuart Gilbert, Collins (The Fontana Library), London 1966. Influential in establishing concept that revolution is primarily social in origin.

ECKSTEIN, HARRY HORACE (ed.), *Internal War, Problems and Approaches*, The Free Press, New York 1964. Brings together strands of current research on generalized political and social violence.

EDWARDS, LYFORD PATERSON, *The Natural History of Revolution*, Russell and Russell, New York 1965 (University of Chicago Sociological Series). Established thesis that 'revolution' was wholly a social phenomenon, most surely approached through the study of 'great revolutions'.

'FREE' (*pseud.* of Abbie Hoffmann), *Revolution for the Hell of It*, The Dial Press, New York 1968. Representative of concept of revolution held by United States youth activists not committed to more traditional ideologies.

GUEVARA, ERNESTO (CHE), *Guerrilla Warfare*, Monthly Review Press, New York and London 1967. Handbook of guerrilla warfare of most immediate practical application, given an additional appeal by death of Guevara himself.

JOHNSON, CHALMERS, *Revolution and the Social System*, The Hoover Institution on War, Revolution and Peace, Stanford University, Stanford 1964 (Hoover Institution Studies 3). Adjusts sociological concept of 'great revolutions' to form broad typology of all revolutions.

LE BON, GUSTAVE, *Psychologie des Foules*, Félix Alcan, Paris 1895. English edn. *The Crowd; a Study of the Popular Mind*, intro. Robert K. Merton, Viking Press, New York 1960.

LENIN, VLADIMIR ILYICH, *State and Revolution*, International Publishers, New York 1968. Justifies 'dictatorship of proletariat', so making possible ideological justification of 'permanence', and strengthening appeal of Marxism.

LOCKE, JOHN, *The Second Treatise of Government* ("An Essay Concerning the True Original, Extent and End of Civil Government") *and a Letter Concerning Toleration*, ed. and intro. J. W. Gough, Basil Blackwell, Oxford 1956. Established concept of revolution as a re-ordering of society after change of government.

MACHIAVELLI, NICCOLÒ, *The Prince*, trs. George Bull, Penguin Books, Harmondsworth, Middlesex 1963. Re-established secular concept of revolution as normal political phenomenon.

MALAPARTE, CURZIO, *Coup d'Etat, the technique of revolution*, trs. Sylvia Saunders, E. P. Dutton and Co., New York 1932. Drawing lessons from Russian revolution, introduced concept that *coup d'état* could be, and was being, used to obtain political power for ideologically directed movements.

MARX, KARL and ENGELS, FRIEDRICH, *Selected Works*, Foreign Languages Publishing House, Moscow 1962, 2 vols. Includes both theses of economic causes of revolution and studies of actual events.

MILTON, JOHN, *The Tenure of Kings and Magistrates*, in *The Works of John Milton*, ed. Rev. John Mitford, W. Pickering, London and Little Brown, Boston 1851. First statement that the will of the people was in itself sufficient justification for revolution.

PAINE, THOMAS, *Rights of Man. Being an Answer to Mr Burke's Attack on the French Revolution*, Dent, London and Dutton, New York 1930. Defence of the right of the people to reorder government at their pleasure.

POLYBIUS, *The Histories*, ed. and trs. W. R. Paton, Heinemann, London and Harvard University Press, Cambridge, Mass. 1922, 4 vols. Introduced theory of cyclical pattern of political change being a closed one, avoidable only by adoption of 'mixed' constitution.

ROUSSEAU, JEAN-JACQUES, *Political Writings*, Nelson, Edinburgh 1953. Formalized Social Contract theory advanced by Locke, providing justification for future revolutions.

SCHRAM, STUART R. (ed.), *The Political Thought of Mao Tse-tung*, Pall Mall, London and Praeger, New York 1963. Principal writings of theorist who adapted Marxism to the peasantry and developed technique of guerrilla warfare.

Sorokin, Pitrim Aleksandrovitch, *Socia and Cultural Dynamics, III; Fluctuation of Social Relationships, War, and Revolution*, American Book Company, New York 1937. First analysis of revolutions and related phenomena to use statistical techniques; relates them to shifts in sociocultural outlook and advances thesis of fluctuating pattern.

The Holy Bible containing the Old and New Testaments translated out of the original tongues: and with the former translations diligently compared and revised, by His Majesty's special command, A.D. 1611, British and Foreign Bible Society, London 1936. Generally regarded as the exemplar of the doctrine of Christian obedience as set forth in the New Testament, but in the Reformation, Old Testament examples were used with equal effect to justify insurrection.

2 Secondary

Calvert, Peter, "Revolution: the Politics of Violence", *Political Studies*, xv, No. 1, February 1967, p. 1. Calls for resumption of work on revolution as a political rather than a social phenomenon.

Friedrich, Carl J. (ed.), *Nomos VII: Revolution*, Atherton Press, New York 1966. Collects essential modern views on the phenomenon.

Hatto, Arthur, "Revolution: An Enquiry into the Usefulness of an Historical Term", *Mind*, 58, October, 1949, p. 495. Valuable collection of observations on the growth of the concept.

Horowitz, Irving Louis (comp.), *The Rise and Fall of Project Camelot; studies in the relationship between social science and practical politics*, M.I.T. Press, Cambridge, Mass. 1967. Illustrates problems of social science research in relation to movements of ideological significance.

Leiden, Carl and Schmitt, Karl M., *The Politics of Violence: Revolution in the Modern World*, Prentice-Hall, Englewood-Cliffs, N.J. 1968. Most recent comparative treatment of specific revolutions.

Marcuse, Herbert, *Reason and Revolution; Hegel and the rise of Social theory*, Routledge and Kegan Paul, London 1968, second edition. A critical work that became in turn a statement for a new generation.

Yoder, Dale, "Current Definitions of Revolution", *The American Journal of Sociology*, xxxii, No. 3, November, 1926, p. 433. Useful summary.

General Bibliography

1 Primary

Almond, Gabriel and Coleman, James S., *The Politics of the Developing Areas*, Princeton University Press, Princeton 1960.

Arendt, Hannah, *On Revolution*, Faber and Faber, London 1963.

Augustinus, Aurelius, St, *The City of God*, trs. John Healey, Dent, London and Dutton, New York 1934.

BAKHUNIN, MIKHAIL, *Archives Bakhounine/Bakunin Archiv*, T. Brill, Leiden 1969– for International Instituut voor Sociale Geschiedenis, Amsterdam.

BUDGE, E. A. WALLIS (ed.), *Egyptian Literature*, Vol. 1 : *Legends of the Gods*. Kegan Paul, Trench, Trübner and Co., London 1912.

BUDGE, E. A. WALLIS, *The Papyrus of Ani*, Putnam, New York 1913, 3 vols.

BROGAN, DENIS W., *The Price of Revolution*, Hamish Hamilton, London 1951.

CAESAR, C. JULIUS, *The Civil War*, Penguin Books, Harmondsworth, Middlesex 1967.

CALVERT, PETER, *A Study of Revolution*, Clarendon Press, Oxford, forthcoming.

CALVIN, JEAN, *Institutes of the Christian Religion*, ed. John T. McNeill, trs. Ford Lewis Battles, Westminster Press, Philadelphia 1960.

CHORLEY, KATHARINE C., *Armies and the Art of Revolution*, Faber and Faber, London 1943.

CICERO, MARCUS TULLIUS, *De Re Publica. De Legibus*, trs. C. W. Keyes Heinemann, London and Harvard University Press, Cambridge, Mass. 1951.

―――― *The Speeches*, ed. and trs. Louis E. Lord, Heinemann, London and Harvard University Press, Cambridge, Mass. 1953. PA 6156.

COMMAGER, HENRY STEELE (ed.), *Documents of American History*, Appleton-Century-Crofts, New York 1958.

DEBRAY, RÉGIS, "Latin America: the Long March", *New Left Review*, 33, September–October 1965, p. 17.

―――― *Revolution in the Revolution?* Penguin Books, Harmondsworth, Middlesex 1969.

DENTON, FRANK H. and PHILIPS, WARREN, "Some Patterns in the History of Violence", *The Journal of Conflict Resolution*, XII, No. 2, June 1968, p. 182.

ENGELS, FRIEDRICH, *Anti-Dühring; Herr Eugen Dühring's revolution in science*, Foreign Languages Publishing House, Moscow 1962.

ERMAN, ADOLF, *The Literature of the Ancient Egyptians*, Methuen, London 1927.

FALL, BERNARD B. (ed.), *Ho Chi Minh On Revolution: Selected Writings, 1920–66*, Pall Mall, London 1967.

FANON, FRANTZ, *The Wretched of the Earth*, Penguin Books, Harmondsworth, Middlesex 1967.

FEIERABEND, IVO K. and FEIERABEND, ROSALIND L., "Aggressive Behaviours Within Polities, 1948–1962, a cross-national study", *Journal of Conflict Resolution*, X, No. 3, September 1966, p. 249.

FINER, SAMUEL E., *The Man on Horseback*, Pall Mall, London 1962.

FOUR MASTERS, THE, see O'Clery, Michael, *et al*.

FREUD, SIGMUND, *Group Psychology and the Analysis of the Ego* (1921), trs. James Strachey, Bantam Books, New York 1965.

GARDINER, ALAN H., *The Admonitions of an Egyptian Sage from a Heiratic Papyrus in Leiden* (Pap. Leiden 344 recto), J. C. Hinrich'sche Buchhandlung, Leipzig 1909.

GOODSPEED, D. J., *The Conspirators, A Study of the Coup d'Etat*, Macmillan, London 1962.

GROSS, FELIKS, *The Seizure of Political Power in a Century of Revolutions*, Philosophical Library, New York 1958.

GUEVARA DE LA SERNA, ERNESTO (CHE), *The Complete Bolivian Dairies of Che Guevara and other captured Documents*, ed. and intro. Daniel James, Stein and Day, New York 1968.

HARRINGTON, JAMES, *The Political Writings of James Harrington; Representative Selections*, ed. and intro. Charles Blitzer, Bobbs-Merrill, Indianapolis 1955.

HEGEL, GEORG WILHELM FRIEDRICH, *Hegel's Philosophy of Right*, trs. T. M. Knox, Clarendon Press, Oxford 1962.

HERODOTUS, *Histories*, ed. Henry Cary, G. Bell and Sons, London 1917.

HOFFER, ERIC, *The True Believer: thoughts on the nature of mass movements*, Harper, New York 1951.

IBN KHALDUN, *The Muquaddimah; an introduction to history*, trs. F. Rosenthal, Pantheon Books, New York 1958.

JANOS, ANDREW C., *The Seizure of Power: a study of force and popular consent*, Center of International Studies, Woodrow Wilson School of Public and International Affairs, Princeton University, Research Monograph No. 16, 1964.

JOHN OF SALISBURY, *The Statesman's Book*, . . . selections . . . from the *Policraticus*, Russell and Russell, New York 1963.

KORNHAUSER, WILLIAM, "Revolution and National Development". Paper delivered at Sixth World Congress of Sociology, Evian, 1966.

KROPOTKIN, PETR ALEKSEEVICH, *Memoirs of a Revolutionist*, ed. James Allen Rogers, Doubleday, Garden City, New York 1962.

LASSALLE, FERDINAND JOHANN GOTTLIEB, *Reden und Schriften*, ed. Ludwig Maenner, R. Hobbing, Berlin 1926, 3 vols.

LAWRENCE, THOMAS EDWARD, *The Seven Pillars of Wisdom*, M. Pike with H. J. Hodgson, London 1926.

LENIN, VLADIMIR ILYICH, *Selected Works*, Foreign Languages Publishing House, Moscow 1968, 3 vols.

LUTHER, MARTIN, *Martin Luther: Selections from his Writings*, ed. and intro. John Dillenberger, Doubleday Anchor, Garden City, N.Y. 1961.

LUTTWAK, EDWARD, *Coup d'Etat, a practical handbook*, Allen Lane, The Penguin Press, London 1968.

MACHIAVELLI, NICCOLÒ, *The Prince and the Discourses*, Random House, New York 1950.

MAO TSE-TUNG and GUEVARA, ERNESTO (CHE), *Guerrilla Warfare*, Cassell, London 1964.

MARSILIUS OF PADUA, *The Defender of Peace* (The *Defensor Pacis*), trs. Alan Gewirth, Harper Torchbooks, New York 1956.

MARTÍ, JOSÉ, *The America of José Martí: selected writings*, trs. Juan de Onís, Funk and Wagnalls, New York 1968.

MAZZINI, GIUSEPPE, *The Duties of Man and other essays by Joseph Mazzini*, Dent, London and Dutton, New York 1912.

NASUTION, ABDUL HARIS, *Fundamentals of Guerrilla Warfare*, facsimile ed., intro. Otto Heilbrunner, Praeger. New York 1965.

NEUMANN, SIGMUND, *Permanent Revolution; Totalitarianism in the Age of International Civil War*, Pall Mall, London 1965. Second edn. of *Permanent Revolution: the Total State in a World at War*, Harper, New York 1942.

NKRUMAH, KWAME, *Handbook of Revolutionary Warfare; a guide to the armed phase of the African Revolution*, Panaf Books, London 1968.

O'CLERY, MICHAEL, et al., *Annals of the Kingdom of Ireland by the Four Masters from the Earliest Period to the year 1616*, trs. J. O'Donovan, Hodges and Smith, Dublin 1851, 7 vols.

PETTEE, GEORGE SAWYER, *The Process of Revolution*, Harper Brothers, New York 1938.

PLATO, *The Republic of Plato*, trs. F. M. Cornford, Clarendon Press, Oxford 1955.

PROUDHON, PIERRE JOSEPH, *Idée générale de la Révolution au xixe siècle*, Garnier, Paris 1851.

RICHARDSON, LEWIS F., *Statistics of Deadly Quarrels*, Stevens and Sons, London 1960.

ROBESPIERRE, MAXIMILIEN MARIE ISIDORE DE, *Oeuvres complètes*, Leroux, Paris 1910–, 10 vols.

ROSENAU, JAMES N. (ed.), *International Aspects of Civil Strife*, Princeton University Press, Princeton 1964.

RUDÉ, GEORGE, *The Crowd in History; A Study of Popular Disturbances in France and England, 1730–1848*, John Wiley and Sons, New York 1964 (New Dimensions in History).

SARMIENTO, DOMINGO FAUSTINO, *Life in the Argentine Republic in the Days of the Tyrants, or, Civilization and Barbarism*, Collier, New York 1961.

SMELSER, NEIL J., *Theory of Collective Behavior*, Routledge and Kegan Paul, London 1962.

SOREL, GEORGES, *Reflections on Violence*, trs. T. E. Hulme and J. Roth; intro. Edward A. Shils, The Free Press, Glencoe, Ill. 1950.

SOROKIN, PITRIM A[leksandrovitch], *The Sociology of Revolution*, J. B. Lippincott Company, Philadelphia and London 1925.

SUETONIUS TRANQUILLUS, GAIUS, *The Twelve Caesars*, trs. Robert Graves, Penguin Books, Harmondsworth, Middlesex 1958.

TACITUS, PUBLIUS CORNELIUS, *The Annals of Imperial Rome*, trs. and intro. Michael Grant, Penguin Books, Harmondsworth, Middlesex 1956.

TANTER, RAYMOND and MIDLARSKY, MANUS, "A Theory of Revolution", *The Journal of Conflict Resolution*, XI, No. 3, September 1967, p. 264.

THOREAU, HENRY DAVID, *Walden and 'Civil Disobedience'*, New American Library, Signet, New York 1960.

THUCYDIDES, *The Peloponnesian War*, trs. Rex Warner, Penguin Books, Harmondsworth, Middlesex 1956.

TILLY, CHARLES and RULE, JAMES, *Measuring Political Upheaval*, Center of International Studies, Woodrow Wilson School of Public and International Affairs, Princeton University, 1965, Research Monograpy No. 19.

TROTSKY, LEON, *History of the Russian Revolution to Brest-Litovsk*, Gollancz, London 1966.

TRUONG CHINH (*pseud.* of Dang Xuan Khu), *Primer for Revolt, the Communist Takeover in Viet-Nam*, facsimile edition of *The August Revolution and the Resistance Will Win*, intro. and notes, Bernard B. Fall, Praeger, New York 1963.

VASCONCELOS, JOSÉ, *¿ Que es la revolución ?*, ed. Botas, Mexico City 1937.

VO NGUYEN GIAP, *People's War, People's Army*, Praeger, New York 1965, 2nd edn.

WOLFENSTEIN, E. VICTOR, *The Revolutionary Personality: Lenin, Trotsky, Gandhi*, Princeton University Press, Princeton 1967.

2 Secondary

AMANN, PETER (ed.), *The Eighteenth-Century Revolution, French or Western ?*, D. C. Heath, Boston, 1963.

—— "Revolution: A Redefinition", *Political Science Quarterly*, LXXVII, 1, March, 1962, p. 36.

ANDREWES, A., *The Greek Tyrants*, Hutchinson University Library, London 1958.

BANKS, ARTHUR S. and TEXTOR, ROBERT, *A Cross-Polity Survey*, Harvard University Press, Cambridge, Mass. 1963.

BAYNES, NORMAN H., *The Political Ideas of St. Augustine's "De Civitate Dei"*, The Historical Association, London 1957.

BLACK, CYRIL E. and THORNTON, THOMAS P., *Communism and Revolution, The Strategic Uses of Political Violence*, Princeton University Press, Princeton 1964.

BRINK, C. O. and WALBANK, F. W., "The Construction of the Sixth Book of Polybius", *The Classical Quarterly*, New Series, IV, No. 3, 4, July–October 1954, p. 97.

CALVERT, PETER, "The Institutionalization of the Mexican Revolution", *Journal of Inter-American Studies*, XI, No. 4, October 1969, p. 503.

CAULFIELD, MAX, *The Easter Rebellion*, Four Square, London 1965.

COWELL, FRANK RICHARD, *Cicero and the Roman Republic*, Penguin Books, Harmondsworth, Middlesex 1956.

DAVIES, JAMES C., "Towards a Theory of Revolution", *American Sociological Review*, XXVII, No. 1, February, 1962, p. 5.

DUTT, R. PALME, *Fascism and Social Revolution; A Study of the Economics and Politics of the Extreme Stages of Capitalism in Decay*, International Publishers, New York 1935, revised edn.

FERRARI, GIUSEPPE, *Teoria dei periodi politici*, Milano-Napoli 1874.

FRANKFORT, HENRI, FRANKFORT, MRS H. A., WILSON, JOHN A. and JACOBSEN, THORKILD, *Before Philosophy; the intellectual adventure of ancient man*, Penguin Books, Harmondsworth, Middlesex 1963.

GASPAR, ELISEO RANGEL, *Hacia una Teoria de la Revolución Mexicana*, Talleres Graficos de la Nación, Mexico City 1964.

GOTTSCHALK, LOUIS, "Leon Trotsky and the Natural History of Revolutions", *The American Journal of Sociology*, XLIV, No. 3, November 1938, p. 339.

JOHNSON, CHALMERS, *Revolutionary Change*, Little, Brown and Co., Boston 1966.

JOLL, JAMES, *The Anarchists*, Eyre and Spottiswoode, London 1964.

LASSWELL, HAROLD D., *Politics: Who gets What, When, How*, The World Publishing Co., Cleveland and New York 1958.

——— *Psychopathology and Politics*, Viking Press, New York 1960.

LASSWELL, HAROLD D. and LERNER, DANIEL (eds), *World Revolutionary Elites: Studies in Coercive Ideological Movements*, The M.I.T. Press, Cambridge, Mass. 1966.

LATHAM, R. C., "English Revolutionary Thought", *History*, New Series, XXX, 1945, p. 38.

LEWIS, ANTHONY, and the staff of the *New York Times, Portrait of a Decade; the Second American Revolution*, Bantam Books, New York 1965.

LINTOTT, A. W., *Violence in Republican Rome*, Clarendon Press, Oxford 1968.

LUKACS, JOHN A., *Decline and Rise of Europe, a study in recent history with particular emphasis on the development of a European consciousness*, Doubleday, Garden City, New York 1965.

McDONALD, JOAN, *Rousseau and the French Revolution, 1762–1791*, University of London, The Athlone Press, London 1965.

MEISEL, ALFRED, "Revolution and Counter-Revolution", *Encyclopedia of the Social Sciences*, 1934.

MEISEL, JAMES H., *Pareto and Mosca*, Prentice-Hall, Englewood-Cliffs, N.J. 1965 (Makers of Modern Social Science).

MELOTTI, UMBERTO, *Rivoluzione e Società*, Ed. La Culturale, Milano 1965.

MERTON, ROBERT K., *Contemporary Social Problems; an introduction to the sociology of deviant behaviour and social disorganization*. Harcourt, Brace and World, New York 1961.

NEEDLER, MARTIN C., "Mexico, Revolution as a Way of Life", in his *Political Systems of Latin America*, Van Nostrand, New York 1964.

PARET, PETER and SHY, JOHN W., *Guerrillas in the 1960s*, Praeger, New York 1962, revised edn.

PUSTAY, JOHN W., *Counterinsurgency Warfare*, Free Press, New York and Collier–Macmillan, London 1965.

QUIRK, ROBERT E., *The Mexican Revolution, 1914–1915; The Convention of Aguascalientes*, Indiana University Press, Bloomington 1960.

RAPOPORT, DAVID C., "Coup d'Etat, the View of the Men Firing Pistols", *Nomos VII: Revolution*, ed. Carl J. Friedrich, Atherton Press, New York, 1966.

ROBERTSON, PRISCILLA, *Revolutions of 1848, a social history*, Harper, New York 1960.

ROSENTHAL, ERWIN I. J., *Political Thought in Medieval Islam, an introductory outline*, Cambridge University Press, Cambridge 1962.

RUSSETT, BRUCE M., *World Handbook of Political and Social Indicators*, Yale University Press, New Haven 1964.

SCHEER, ROBERT and ZEITLIN, MAURICE, *Cuba, an American Tragedy*, Penguin Books, Harmondsworth, Middlesex 1964, rev. edn.

SEALE, PATRICK and McCONVILLE, MAUREEN, *French Revolution, 1968*, Penguin Books, Harmondsworth, Middlesex 1969.

STONE, LAWRENCE, "Theories of Revolution", *World Politics*, XVIII, No. 2, January 1966, p. 159.

SYME, SIR R., *The Roman Revolution*, Clarendon Press, Oxford 1939.

THAYER, CHARLES W., *Guerrilla*, Michael Joseph, London 1963.

ULLMAN, WALTER, *A History of Political Thought: The Middle Ages*, Penguin Books, Harmondsworth, Middlesex 1965.

VITTACHI, TARZIE, *The Fall of Sukarno*, Praeger, New York 1967.

WALBANK, F. W., "Polybius on the Roman Constitution", *The Classical Quarterly*, XXXVII, No. 3, 4, July–October 1943, p. 73.

WEDGWOOD, C. V., *William the Silent. William of Nassau, Prince of Orange, 1533–1584*, Jonathan Cape, London 1944.

3 Additional background sources used

ADORNO, T. W., BRUNSWIK-FRENKEL, ELSE, LEVINSON, DANIEL J. and SANFORD, R. NEVITT, *The Authoritarian Personality*, John Wiley, New York 1964, 2 vols.

BREASTED, JAMES HENRY, *The Dawn of Conscience*, Scribner, New York 1934.

—— *A History of Egypt, from the Earliest Times to the Persian Conquest*, Hodder and Stoughton, London 1951, second edn.

BRENAN, GERALD, *The Spanish Labyrinth, an account of the Social and Political Background of the Spanish Civil War*, Cambridge University Press, Cambridge 1962.

BUTTERFIELD, L. H., "July 4 in 1826", *American Heritage*, VI, 4, p. 14.

DE GRAZIA, SEBASTIAN, *The Political Community, a study of anomie*, The University of Chicago Press Chicago (Phoenix Books), 1963.

DURKHEIM, EMILE, *The Division of Labor in Society*, trs. George Simpson, The Free Press, New York 1965.

EMERSON, RALPH WALDO, *Essays: First and Second Series*, A. L. Burt, New York, undated.

EMERY, WALTER B., *Archaic Egypt*, Penguin Books, Harmondsworth, Middlesex 1961.

FERRER GUARDIA, FRANCISCO, *The Origin and Ideas of the Modern School*, trs. Joseph McCabe, G. P. Putnam, New York 1913.

GARDINER, SIR ALAN, *Egypt of the Pharaohs, an Introduction*, Clarendon Press, Oxford 1961.

GOLDMAN, EMMA, *Anarchism and Other Essays*, The Mother Earth Publishing Association, New York 1910.

GREEN, ALICE STOPFORD, *History of the Irish State to 1014*, Macmillan and Co., London 1925.

KEYNES, JOHN MAYNARD, *The Economic Consequences of the Peace*, Macmillan, London 1920.

LEFF, GORDON, *Medieval Thought from Saint Augustine to Ockham*, Penguin Books, Harmondsworth, Middlesex 1958.

MAIR, LUCY, *Primitive Government*, Penguin Books, Harmondsworth, Middlesex 1962.

MONTGOMERY, RUTH, *A Gift of Prophecy; the Phenomenal Jeane Dixon*, William Morrow, New York 1965.

NKRUMAH, KWAME, *Neocolonialism; the Last Stage of Imperialism*, Nelson, London 1965.

RAPHAEL (pseud.), *Raphael's Prophetic Almanack for 1917*, W. Foulsham, London 1916.

RICHARDS, VERNON, *Errico Malatesta, his Life and Ideas*, Freedom Press, London 1965.

SHINNIE, PETER L., *Meroe, a Civilization of the Sudan*, Thames and Hudson, London 1967.

SPENCER, HERBERT, *Principles of Sociology*, abridged ed. Stanislav Andreski, Archon Books, Hamden, Conn. 1969.

TACITUS, PUBLIUS CORNELIUS, *On Britain and Germany*, trs. and intro. H. Mattingly, Penguin Books, Harmondsworth, Middlesex 1951.

VAGTS, ALFRED, *A History of Militarism, Civilian and Military*, Hollis and Carter, London 1959.

VALLENILLA LANZ, LAUREANO, *Cesarismo democrático*, Caracas 1919.

WEBER, MAX, *The Theory of Social and Economic Organization*, ed. and intro. Talcott Parsons, The Free Press, New York 1965.

WEIGALL, ARTHUR, *The Glory of the Pharaohs*, Thornton Butterworth, London 1936.

Index